IRONCLAD IN CHRIST JESUS

Rohit Phillips

ISBN 979-8-89345-366-9 (paperback)
ISBN 979-8-89345-367-6 (digital)

Copyright © 2024 by Rohit Phillips

All rights reserved. No part of this publication may be reproduced, distributed, or transmitted in any form or by any means, including photocopying, recording, or other electronic or mechanical methods without the prior written permission of the publisher. For permission requests, solicit the publisher via the address below.

Christian Faith Publishing
832 Park Avenue
Meadville, PA 16335
www.christianfaithpublishing.com

"Scripture quotations taken from The AMPLIFIED Bible, Copyright © 1954, 1958, 1962, 1964, 1965, 1987, 2015 by The Lockman Foundation. All rights reserved. Used by permission." (www.Lockman.org)

Printed in the United States of America

To my loving mother, Avis Promila Dwyer; my beloved wife, Meghna; and precious daughters, Twisha and Rhea.

Contents

Acknowledgment vii
Preface ix
Believer or Not 1
Discipline and Training 4
Obedience 10
Read and Meditate on the Word 14
Faith Is an Act 23
    Faith Needs to Be Qualified 27
    Faith Is a Muscle 31
    Faith Is a Fight 32
Love Walk 35
Prayer Life 41
    Prayer in Tongues 46
Authority of Believers to Lead Abundant Lives 49
    Believer's Authority over Health 51
    Believer's Authority to Get Wealth 63
    Believer's Authority to Be Peaceful 71

Acknowledgment

This book is a result of sitting under the Word at my local church and the revelations that were poured into me by God through many hours of praying in the Holy Spirit, wrestling with God, and being taken up to heaven by Jesus in His loving embrace on January 11, 2024, at 7:00 a.m.

I thank all the pastors who have taught the Word of God now for over fifty years of my life and I am eternally grateful to Jesus Christ for saving me.

Preface

Growing up in a nominal Christian home and attending Church regularly, I have always marveled at the great men and women of God who bring God's Word and healing with so much power and authority. Even the men and women of God mentioned in the Bible seem to have God's special blessings and flow in such power and have made many conquests in the natural and spiritual. Observing all these successful people can put a feeling of unworthiness or failure in normal Christians going about their lives doing secular jobs or carrying on with their day-to-day lives. After all, didn't the Lord command just before ascending to heaven saying,

> All authority (all power of rule) in heaven and on earth has been given to Me. Go then and make disciples of all nations, baptizing them in the name of the Father and of the Son and of the Holy Spirit, Teaching them to observe everything that I have commanded you, and behold, I am with you all the days (perpetually, uniformly, and on every occasion), to the [very] end *and consummation* of the age. *Amen (so let it be)*." (Matthew 28:18–20 AMPC)

Surely, the pastors and evangelists are doing exactly that, devoting their lives to the work of God. But what about the majority of us who sit in the pews of Churches all our lives and just go about living our lives as homemakers, office workers, or carrying on some business? How do our lives matter in the kingdom? At the end of our journey on earth, will we also hear the Lord say, "Well done, you upright (honorable, admirable) and faithful servant! You have been faithful *and* trustworthy over a little; I will put you in charge of much. Enter into and share the joy (the delight, the blessedness) which your master enjoys." (Matthew 25:21 AMPC).

If you have had such thoughts too like me, then I would like to encourage you to continue reading. This book is an attempt to unfold what God has in His mind for people like you and me who are not called to be ministers or pastors in the sense of it being our vocation. We have the same power and authority available to us as any apostle, prophet, evangelist, pastor, or teacher to not just lead fruitful lives for ourselves but to bring about God's love and blessings into the lives of people around us. The Bible says, "But you are a chosen race, a royal priesthood, a dedicated nation, [God's] own purchased, special people, that you may set forth the wonderful deeds and display the virtues and perfections of Him Who called you out of darkness into His marvelous light" (1 Peter 2:9 AMPC).

Believer or Not

A Christian can either be a believer in Christ Jesus and His supremacy or a doubter of His sovereignty. The latter is a dangerous place to be in. If a person says he is a Christian but lives a life buffeted by sickness, disease, addictions, and slavery to worldly passions, then there is no difference between him and a nonbeliever. We all face these issues in our lives every now and then, but we do not have to stay bound to these afflictions. Sadly, most Christians live like nonbelievers and hence lead unfruitful lives, for Jesus said, "I am the Vine; you are the branches. Whoever lives in Me and I in him bears much (abundant) fruit. However, apart from Me [cut off from vital union with Me] you can do nothing" (John 15:5 AMPC).

So if we are living unfruitful lives, then we are cut off from Jesus. But we do not have to continue living defeated lives if we have accepted Jesus Christ as our personal Savior. All that is required is to take every Word in the Bible at face value, believe it wholeheartedly, and do it.

> Every Scripture is God-breathed (given by His inspiration) and profitable for instruction, for reproof and conviction of sin, for correction of error and discipline in obedience, [and] for training in righteousness (in holy living, in conformity to God's will in thought, purpose, and action). (2 Timothy 3:16 AMPC)

Either the Bible is the truth or a lie. We cannot read the Bible and then the next moment live our lives as though what we read in the Bible does not apply to our daily lives.

I have been guilty of living for a long time in addiction to alcohol and smoking even though I was born and brought up in a "Christian home." I put "Christian home" in quotes because just the label of Christianity does not make a person or family "believers." I saw my dad from childhood into these addictions, and I think picking up these habits was easy for me in high school. My parents separated during this crucial period of my life, and that further gave me a justification in the back of my head to lead my life as I pleased without much accountability. A large chunk of my growing up years were with my mother who took up the responsibility to bring up my elder brother and me. The 1970s and '80s were not the easiest years especially in a third-world country like India (in those days) for a woman to raise a family alone. The economic and social challenges were enough for my mother to manage, so bringing us up with Christian values took a back seat. She did extremely well in inculcating good values in us, but there is a difference between good values and Christian values. Good worldly values say, "Love your friends," but Jesus said, "Love your enemies." Good values say, "Save for a rainy day," but Jesus said, "Give and it shall be given to you pressed down, shaken together, flowing over." I have always appreciated and valued my mother for her unconditional love and responsibility toward bringing up my brother and me.

The point is that sometimes, life does throw challenges at us in ways that separate us from growing into the full potential of being powerful Christians. But I believe everyone gets a chance as they come to the age of accountability, to change course and accept Jesus in their lives. Whether they have heard about Jesus from someone or have grown up in nominal Christian homes, God gives everyone a chance to accept Jesus. In fact, this age (the Church Age) will not end until everyone has heard the message of Jesus Christ and then Jesus will come back with judgment.

"And this good news of the kingdom (the Gospel) will be preached throughout the whole world as a testimony to all the nations, and then will come the end" (Matthew 24:14 AMPC).

IRONCLAD IN CHRIST JESUS

So what do we do once we have heard and accepted Jesus as our Lord and Savior? How do we start living the *ironclad, powerful, surefire* life that Jesus promises?

> And these attesting signs will accompany those who believe: in My name they will drive out demons; they will speak in new languages; They will pick up serpents; and [even] if they drink anything deadly, it will not hurt them; they will lay their hands on the sick, and they will get well.
> (Mark 16:17–18 AMPC)

Discipline and Training

> You must submit to and endure [correction] for *discipline*; God is dealing with you as with sons. For what son is there whom his father does not [thus] train and correct and *discipline*? (Hebrews 12:7 AMPC)

I always wanted to drive a car. Looking at people driving so easily with one hand on the steering wheel and turning sharp turns or navigating narrow lanes with such ease, I felt I could drive without any training. Once my brother's friend offered me to drive his car after coming out of a bar in high spirits! I gladly accepted the offer and started confidently, only to realize the next moment that we had hit a road median. Then after many years of driving in India, I came to Canada and failed the road test three times before realizing that I had to unlearn a lot and adapt to a new set of driving rules and environment.

Discipline and training are as important in our spiritual walk as in natural education, training, and experience. We must look at our lives through the lens of the Word of God (Bible) and make a note of every area where we need to change or make corrections or learn new skills. I was a habitual smoker and occasional drinker, but after starting my working life, someone introduced me to the monthly magazine *Every Day with Jesus* by Selwyn Hughes. Every morning, I would read the day's reading and God started answering my questions and addressing my struggles specific to what I was dealing with the previous day. Jesus started filling the void of the natural father's love and care that I had missed growing up.

Over time, I started developing a desire to stop smoking and drinking, but as the joke goes, quitting these bad habits was quite easy for me. I had quit several times over many years!

But our loving Father does not give up on His children, and He put a desire in my heart to serve Him. This became my regular prayer that Jesus would use me for His glory. I would seek forgiveness in the morning for smoking the previous day and then find myself with a cigarette outside my workplace or drinking with friends in the evening occasionally. Then after several years of trying and failing, one morning in 2009, I again said, "Lord, I want to serve you." And this passage from the Bible struck me like a tight slap on my face:

> And Joshua said to the people, You cannot serve the Lord, for He is a holy God; He is a jealous God. He will not forgive your transgressions or your sins.
> And the people said to Joshua, No; but we will serve the Lord. Then Joshua said to the people, You are witnesses against yourselves that you have chosen the Lord, to serve Him. And they said, We are witnesses. (Joshua 24:19, 21–22 AMPC)

It's that day in 2009 that I developed a hatred toward even the smell of cigarettes, let alone picking one up to bring to my lips that are reserved to only praise our living Lord Jesus Christ.

"Do you not know that your body is the temple (the very sanctuary) of the Holy Spirit Who lives within you, Whom you have received [as a Gift] from God?" (1 Corinthians 6:19 AMPC).

Discipline and training are a lifelong thing for believers. You do not have to wait till fully trained to serve the Lord, for we are all being transformed into the image of Christ over our lifetime.

> And all of us, as with unveiled face, [because we] continued to behold [in the Word of God] as in a mirror the glory of the Lord, are constantly

being transfigured into His very own image in ever increasing splendor and from one degree of glory to another; [for this comes] from the Lord [Who is] the Spirit. (2 Corinthians 3:18 AMPC)

You graduate from being a rookie to an officer to a lieutenant and then to a general and so on. You can start experiencing little victories in the spiritual realms even as a rookie. I used to be in the last seven in my class of about fifty as a kid, and in those days, you had to go to school with your parents to pick up the final report card for the school year. It used to be the most dreadful day for me even though my parents never reprimanded me for my academic misdemeanors as they just expected me to make it to the next grade. I remember that morning when we were going to pick up my grade 9 report card. I went to the prayer altar on top of the fireplace in our living room, which had the cross with some flower petals around it. Without much spiritual understanding, I simply went and prayed to Jesus, picked up a petal from the feet of Jesus's cross, and ate it, believing that it would supernaturally bump me into the next grade. As I was walking from the parking lot to my classroom, kids from my class were staring at me. My heart pounding in my chest, I thought *Did I even drop out of the league of the last seven?* Then we were greeted by my teacher with a big congratulations. I stood first in the class! Oh, how the Lord bestows His supernatural favor when we humble ourselves and go to Him in complete surrender! Now, don't get me wrong. I am not saying that prayer and faith are the easy way out of human effort and work. Rather, prayer and faith surely can bring divine favor and blessings into our daily lives that will get us supernatural results and the abundant life that Jesus promises.

God disciplines and trains everyone differently as He knows the plans for our lives.

"For I know the thoughts and plans that I have for you, says the Lord, thoughts and plans for welfare and peace and not for evil, to give you hope in your final outcome" (Jeremiah 29:11 AMPC).

You will start experiencing the spiritual gifts available to you as you humble yourself daily in the presence of the Lord and read His

Word. The Holy Spirit will lead you gently and train you in the specific areas He wants to use you in.

Before I knew about the spiritual gifts available to me, the Holy Spirit was leading me through my life experiences to become skillful in these areas. I was in the early years of my working life in Bangalore with a paltry salary enough to give a decent life to my wife and our firstborn child who had not yet learned to walk. One of my biological dad's friends called from a different city (Allahabad) where my dad lived, bringing the news that my dad was severely ill and in the hospital. I flew there and soon learned that my dad had slipped into a coma, and the hospital wanted him to be shifted to a bigger hospital as they could not do anything more to save his life. I waited for my elder brother Amit to join us, and then we moved our dad to a bigger hospital in a different city (Lucknow) where we reached in the evening and were told that very little could be done to save his life. The junior doctor on duty admitted him. In the meanwhile, he said that his back could be patted on either side. Dad was in the hospital in a comatose state for three days and the doctors mentioned that there was not much that could be done to save his life as his condition started worsening with blood starting to come out in his urine.

My brother and I took turns to be with Dad, and it was my turn to be with him on the third night. I sat beside my dad patting his back and praying throughout the night. I was crying and praying the whole night, asking God that my dad should not die this time as I had hardly any money to give him a decent funeral. Without knowing the spiritual principles involved in raising someone from the dead (almost dead in this case), the Holy Spirit led me to make my vessel (body, soul, and spirit) available to intercede for my dad's life. In the current dispensation (Church age), all authority on earth to bring about the plans of God to fruition has been given to the body of Christ (the Church) by Jesus (who is the Head). As one of the greatest modern-day apostles, Kenneth E. Hagin said the following: First, as soon as Jesus said, *"All power (or authority) is given unto me in heaven and in earth,"* He immediately delegated that authority on earth to the Church when He said, "Go ye therefore"[1] (Matthew 28:18–19).

God cannot do anything on earth without His children (the Church) praying and making their vessels available to pull the blessings of God from the spiritual realm into the natural. Like the head cannot do anything without the body that is connected to it, in the same way, Christ (the Head) cannot do anything on earth without His body (the Church) working with Him according to His will in the Father (more on this to follow in the chapter on prayer life).

> By having the eyes of your heart flooded with light, so that you can know and understand the hope to which He has called you, and how rich is His glorious inheritance in the saints (His set-apart ones),
>
> And [so that you can know and understand] what is the *immeasurable and unlimited and surpassing greatness of His power in and for us who believe*, as demonstrated in the working of His mighty strength,
>
> Which He exerted in Christ when He raised Him from the dead and seated Him at His [own] right hand in the heavenly [places],
>
> Far above all rule and authority and power and dominion and every name that is named [above every title that can be conferred], not only in this age and in this world, but also in the age and the world which are to come.
>
> *And He has put all things under His feet and has appointed Him the universal and supreme Head of the church* [a headship exercised throughout the church],
>
> Which is His body, the fullness of Him Who fills all in all [for in that body lives the full mea-

---

[1] Kenneth E. Hagin, *Tongues Beyond the Upper Room*, 320.

> *sure of Him Who makes everything complete, and Who fills everything everywhere with Himself].* (Ephesians 1:18–23 AMPC)

So you see in these verses that Jesus has all the power, and He is seated on the right hand of the Father. If He (the Head) is seated at the right hand of the Father in heaven, then we (the church), His body, are also seated with Him and enjoy the same power that Jesus has in heaven and on earth. You cannot separate the head from the body. The head needs the body to function and vice versa. If you don't believe me, then try telling your head to go pick up an apple and eat.

The hospital ward where my dad was admitted had all the terminally ill patients, and the atmosphere was dark and gloomy. But I was engrossed in interceding for my dad's life. And in the morning, my dad opened his eyes, sat up, and kept talking nonstop! When the senior doctor and his team of medical students came to visit Dad, he was surprised at the miraculous recovery. The people in the neighboring beds said that they had only seen patients being taken to the morgue from that ward, and here we were seeing the miracle of God taking our dad home discharged the very same day. Glory to God!

Training and discipline go hand in hand with God and not necessarily in any sequence. But they certainly are extremely important ingredients for believers to start living in the authority of Christ in their daily lives and achieve greater victories for themselves and others.

Obedience

[God] said, Take now your son, your only son Isaac, whom you love, and go to the region of Moriah; and offer him there as a burnt offering upon one of the mountains of which I will tell you.
So Abraham rose early in the morning, saddled his donkey, and took two of his young men with him and his son Isaac; and he split the wood for the burnt offering, and then began the trip to the place of which God had told him. (Genesis 22:2–3 AMPC)

This passage in the Bible has intrigued me a lot on the test that God placed before Abraham to sacrifice his only son that he got as a promise from God when he and Sarah were beyond their childbearing ages at one hundred and ninety years old, respectively. More than the preposterous demand by God, I am amazed at the obedience of Abraham. Without questioning or thinking twice, he got up the next morning and took his only son to sacrifice him. The Bible does not mention any conversation about this between Abraham and Sarah, but I am sure Abraham would have remained silent, or else, Sarah would have slapped his faith out of him and never allowed him to do what he was going to do.

Such obedience can only come from a point of unshakable faith in a good God who could never go against his initial promise to Abraham of giving him descendants as numerous as the stars in the sky.

> And He brought him outside [his tent into the starlight] and said, Look now toward the heavens and count the stars—if you are able to number them. Then He said to him, So shall your descendants be.
>
> And he [Abram] believed in (trusted in, relied on, remained steadfast to) the Lord, and He counted it to him as righteousness (right standing with God). (Genesis 15:5–6 AMPC)

I believe obedience ranks very high in the heart of God as throughout the Old Testament time, God was displeased from time to time with the Israelites due to their disobedience. Even we, like the Israelites, fail to flow in the perfect will of God for our lives now and then by either going our way or just plain disobedience. If we get into doing our own thing without explicitly getting into sin, then God allows us in His grace but then we are in His permissible will, not perfect will. The results are always far from being perfect and fruitful. Early on in my career, God put a desire in me to do business and trained me with all the skills needed to run an advertising agency business by taking me through four large Indian companies and roles over the first four years of my working life, that included product management (Cadila Pharma), corporate communication (Sartorius), advertising sales (DDB Mudra), and team management (Maa Bozell).

God found me ready after the fourth job to start my advertising business, but I wanted to get one more experience in a multinational company. So God allowed me to do what I wanted, but this was not His perfect will for me but His permissible will. Now as I look back, I can understand why I never was able to find my feet in this multinational company (Volvo), and within six months, I resigned. At that time, this greatly discouraged me, and I lost time and my savings as the only earning member in the family. The struggle that followed in putting food on the table for my family was not the perfect will of God for us, as by then, my wife was pregnant with our second child, and I was without any earnings. But God, in His mercy, brought me back in His perfect will by strengthening me to start the advertising business from a room in our home in 2006, which we named Fahrenheit Communications. The company is still in existence and is run by a friend who bought it after we moved to Canada in 2015. That's the fruit of the perfect will of God.

The financial blessings that flowed to us through Fahrenheit took us on vacations across the world to fourteen countries, and we finally settled in Canada, which is by far one of the best countries in the world. What God started through me in a room has continued to survive even after I moved out of the business in 2015. Such are the blessings of God when we flow in His perfect will that its power does not wear off even after His children move out into the next phase of His plan for their lives!

Like many of us, I learned my lessons through the various failures and successes in my life. Whenever I look back on my life, I marvel at the God who puts the puzzle pieces of our lives in the right places to finish the beautiful picture that He has in His mind before we are conceived in our mother's womb.

> For You did form my inward parts; You did knit me together in my mother's womb.
>
> I will confess and praise You for You are fearful and wonderful and for the awful wonder of my birth! Wonderful are Your works, and that my inner self knows right well.
>
> My frame was not hidden from You when I was being formed in secret [and] intricately and curiously wrought [as if embroidered with various colors] in the depths of the earth [a region of darkness and mystery].
>
> Your eyes saw my unformed substance, and in Your book all the days [of my life] were written before ever they took shape, when as yet there was none of them. (Psalm 139:13–16 AMPC)

Whether the complete picture of the puzzle finishes or how long it takes to finish depends on us. We can delay or hinder its completion by disobeying God from time to time or completely abort it by moving out of His will completely. Judas Iscariot, one of the twelve disciples of Jesus, started well by following Him but lost it on the way by betraying Jesus and ended up committing suicide (Acts 1:18).

Read and Meditate on the Word

> IN THE beginning [before all time] was the Word (Christ), and the Word was with God, and the Word was God Himself.
> He was present originally with God.
> All things were made *and* came into existence through Him; and without Him was not even one thing made that has come into being.
> In Him was Life, and the Life was the Light of men.
> And the Light shines on in the darkness, for the darkness has never overpowered it. (John 1:1–5 AMPC)

In the light of these verses, the next time when you pick up your Bible, you know you are reading and meditating on Jesus because Jesus is the Word.

> And the Word (Christ) became flesh (human, incarnate) and tabernacled (fixed His tent of flesh, lived awhile) among us; and we [actually] saw His glory (His honor, His majesty), such glory as an only begotten son receives from his father, full of grace (favor, loving-kindness) and truth. (John 1:14 AMPC)

We can read the Bible as the written word (logos) and nothing much changes in our lives. *Logos* ("word, discourse, or reason") is a term used in Western philosophy, psychology, and rhetoric; it connotes an appeal to rational discourse that relies on inductive and deductive reasoning. It is like reading about Jesus as a historical figure, but there is no relationship building between Him and us. It may be of value to understand the heart and mind of God and even help us develop spiritually. We may become knowledgeable about the triune Godhead (the Father, the Son, and the Holy Spirit) and Christianity as a religion. But what good is that knowledge if we cannot take it to the bank? That is, if that knowledge cannot help us get our healing from sicknesses or diseases of various kinds or financial blessings for our daily needs or answers to prayers, then what good is that knowledge? Still, a majority of Christian folks live their whole lives reading the Bible many times or sitting in Church pews, but nothing much changes in their lives. They may be saved and go to heaven when they die, but their whole life on earth is lived ordinarily without the power of God manifesting on a daily basis.

But when we read the Bible as the revealed Word (*rhema*), then things turn out not just differently; but we start experiencing the power of God in the way we think, speak, and act. *Rhema* literally means an "utterance" or "thing said" in Greek. It is a word that signifies the *action of utterance. Rhema or the revealed word of God is word in action.* We can read a Bible verse as a logos word, and it remains in the mental arena and may be good for reasoning or debate for our own understanding of God or pointing an unbeliever to God. But when we meditate on it till it floats down into our spirit as revealed or rhema word, then we can act upon it because we can now trust it with our life. Now the word becomes useful to change our own lives or circumstances or help someone else. A relationship with the living Word (Jesus) starts to develop. And like any relationship, the more time we spend with the other person, the closer and more enriched our relationship becomes.

We can read the Bible at our home, but it always benefits and is a requirement by God that we join a local church and sit under the office of the pastor as the Word is preached under the anointing of the Holy Spirit. We have to be careful and find a local church where the *rhema* word is preached and not just the *logos* word. A quick check would be to find out if it is a Word and Spirit church where the entire Bible is being preached and not just a few doctrines that are pleasing to the itching ears of the congregation.

I had gone to various churches growing up with my parents but this was just a religious act and out of obedience to my parents. But it was still profitable to me as the logos word was being instilled in me, which helped build a basic understanding of God and what Jesus did for me on the cross. Without me getting a hold of the word my faith was nevertheless slowly building as the Bible says, "So faith comes by hearing [what is told], and what is heard comes by the preaching [of the message that came from the lips] of Christ (the Messiah Himself)" (Romans 10:17 AMPC).

While I was pursuing my postgraduate studies in Bangalore, my soon-to-be wife Meghna introduced me to Koramangala Methodist Church. Here we were deeply impacted by the preaching of Pastor Arun Andrews and Bible study classes by a sweet elderly lady, Auntie Thomas, who was a congregation member at this church. We came close to the person of Jesus Christ and started building a relationship with Him. Thereafter, when I started my first job in Ahmedabad, I made it a habit to read the Bible every morning.

Soon, Meghna and I married, and the Bible started becoming a living Word to us as we started experiencing the hand of our miracle-working God in our lives. One day, after I had resigned from my first job and without earning for a few months, I visited my brother Amit's house for some reason, but he was not at home. The phone rang, and I answered the call. The person on the other side of the call asked for Amit and on introducing myself to take a message on my brother's behalf, the person said that he actually wanted to speak to me. He asked me if I had heard of a company called Sartorius in Bangalore. When I said no, he told me to look it up on the internet and call back if I were interested in attending an interview. But I was so desperate to get a job that I said I don't want to look up and was ready to come over for the interview.

Later, I learned that I was speaking to the managing director of the company who had seen my resume on the internet, which had my aunt Ena Alexander's number who lived in Cochin, Kerala. I had floated my resume on the internet after finishing my postgraduate studies, and since I had no permanent address at that time, I had put her address and phone number on the resume. He had got my brother's number from her as at that time I did not have a phone line in my house, and my aunt knew that both my brother and I lived in the same city. He offered me a first-class to-and-fro train ticket from Ahmedabad to Bangalore to attend the interview. But something in my spirit said that I already got the job, so I asked for a one-way airplane ticket instead as I knew I would not have to come back after the interview. He laughed at my confidence, but after the interview in Bangalore, he offered me the job, and I joined immediately. However, the salary that I had was not enough to find a decent home to get my wife from Ahmedabad. So this gentleman offered to give a job to my wife as well in the human resources department of the company so that with the combined salary we could get a good place to live. This was just the beginning of the financial blessings that God would give us, as we started taking baby steps of faith with The God who provides!

> The LORD is my Shepherd [to feed, guide, and shield me], I shall not lack.
> He makes me lie down in [fresh, tender] green pastures; He leads me beside the still and restful waters.
> He refreshes and restores my life (my self); He leads me in the paths of righteousness [uprightness and right standing with Him—not for my earning it, but] for His name's sake.
> (Psalm 23:1–3 AMPC)

You will experience God's goodness and provisions in every area of your life as you walk in communion with Him and read His word daily to make sure you are not going away from His precepts. And if you move away from Him and get in harm's way like the sheep, which we all do from time to time, then He is our good Shepherd who will comfort us by His staff and drive away the wolves with His rod.

"Yes, though I walk through the [deep, sunless] valley of the shadow of death, I will fear or dread no evil, for You are with me; Your rod [to protect] and Your staff [to guide], they comfort me" (Psalm 23:4 AMPC).

The Bible has everything you will ever need to lead an abundant life. It provides general guidance on matters relating to finance, business, marriage, relationships, health, and even sex. All you need is time to dig into the Word of God about the specific area where you need guidance. And if you need specific counsel and guidance particular to your life's unique issues, then the born-again Spirit-filled believers have the Holy Ghost living inside of them to provide all the answers.

> But when He, the Spirit of Truth (the Truth-giving Spirit) comes, He will guide you into all the Truth (the whole, full Truth). For He will not speak His own message [on His own authority]; but He will tell whatever He hears [from the Father; He will give the message that has been given to Him], and He will announce and declare to you the things that are to come [that will happen in the future]. (John 16:13 AMPC)

Someone might ask how I get this counsel if I am not a believer or if I do believe but don't know if I have the Holy Ghost living inside of me. Now, if you are not a believer, then just repent of your sins and accept Jesus in your heart as Lord and Savior. That's all it takes for you to receive forgiveness of sins and salvation.

"Because if you acknowledge and confess with your lips that Jesus is Lord and in your heart believe (adhere to, trust in, and rely on the truth) that God raised Him from the dead, you will be saved" (Romans 10:9 AMPC).

If you are a Christian but have never experienced the Holy Ghost, then all you need to do is ask the Father for the infilling of the Holy Ghost and believe when you ask. If you don't have enough faith to know that when you ask, then the Father will give you the Holy Ghost then go to a Word and Spirit Church to have hands laid on you for the receiving of the Holy Ghost. Here are the scriptures for both of these cases:

> If you then, evil as you are, know how to give good gifts [gifts that are to their advantage] to your children, how much more will your heavenly Father give the Holy Spirit to those who ask and continue to ask Him! (Luke 11:13 AMPC)

> Then [the apostles] laid their hands on them one by one, and they received the Holy Spirit. (Acts 8:17 AMPC)

I have related earlier that God blessed me with a business, Fahrenheit Communication, in 2006. This is when we were walking in close communion with Him and were running the business as much as we knew according to the principles of business in the Bible. Once, my tax consultant commented that he had hundreds of clients, and I was amongst the very few who paid taxes honestly. I told him about this story from the Bible when the Pharisees were trying to trap Jesus about the matter of paying taxes:

> Tell us then what You think about this: Is it lawful to pay tribute [levied on individuals and to be paid yearly] to Caesar or not?
> But Jesus, aware of their malicious plot, asked, Why do you put Me to the test and try to entrap Me, you pretenders (hypocrites)?
> Show me the money used for the tribute. And they brought Him a denarius.
> And Jesus said to them, Whose likeness and title are these?

> They said, Caesar's. Then He said to them, Pay therefore to Caesar the things that are due to Caesar, and pay to God the things that are due to God. (Matthew 22:17–21 AMPC)

We did the tax part all right but were not very regular on the second part of Jesus's command about giving to God what was due to Him, which is "tithing." While in business, we started attending a church close to our home, and the pastor there, Abraham Alfred, loved us dearly. He once asked me if we were doing our accounting properly with respect to savings for our kids and tithing. I was tithing from the salary that my wife and I were drawing from the business but not on the profits in the business. But the Bible is very clear about giving the first tenth of every increase that God blesses you with and shows the blessing attached to that sacrifice.

> Bring all the tithes (the whole tenth of your income) into the storehouse, that there may be food in My house, and prove Me now by it, says the LORD of hosts, if I will not open the windows of heaven for you and pour you out a blessing, that there shall not be room enough to receive it. (Malachi 3:10 AMPC)

We followed Pastor Abraham's advice to keep our part of the covenant, and God did keep His part of the promise. I related earlier how God prospered us during the nine years that we ran our business and took us around the world on vacations. But here's the part about His opening the windows of heaven to pour out blessings that we did not have room enough to receive.

When my second daughter, Rhea was of school-going age, she developed asthma due to the pollen in the city of Bangalore. The asthma was so severe that we had to rush several times to the hospital in the middle of the night to get her treated for breathlessness. The inhaler was always in her school bag and at every place in our home and cars. We were continuously praying that God would take us out of Bangalore, but the business was well established with about ten to fifteen employees and all debts (home and cars) were paid up, plus there was no better city than Bangalore in India where we could have moved so that our child could be relieved of asthma.

But God was working behind the scenes to prepare a blessing for our family that there would not be room enough to receive. Here's how the Holy Spirit leads and guides you into the blessings of the Father. He prompted me to look at an advertisement in the newspaper about immigration to Canada. I asked my wife to call the number in the advertisement, but she forgot about it. Then some months later, the Holy Spirit again pointed me to a similar advertisement in the newspaper, and I asked my wife if she had made the call. This time we heeded to the Holy Spirit and went to meet the immigration consultant as we had no clue what was involved in this process. The consultant asked a few questions about our educational background and work experience. Then they asked for an initial deposit to start the process. The amount was substantial, but I swiped my credit card, and now there was no turning back. After the payment was made, the consultant gave us a list of documents to work on the application. One of the documents required was our graduation degree certificates, which we had never received from the university to date after more than fifteen years of completing our graduation. To further complicate matters, this university was in a different state, and we had no clue how to get this out now after so many years.

If you have lived in India, you will know that you will need at least one of the 3Ms to get anything out of government-run institutions: money, might, or miracle. As Spirit-filled Christians, we decided that we would not resort to the first M (money) and the second M (might) we had none. So we told God that if you want to take us to Canada, then you will have to work out the third M (miracle). Remember what God said in Malachi 3:10? *"'Test Me now in this,' says the LORD of hosts, 'if I will not open for you the windows of heaven.'"*

So we went ahead with the application process and requested a relative of ours who lived in the same city where this university is to help us with putting a request in the university for both of our degree certificates. To our surprise, the degree certificates arrived at our home by post sent directly by the university. The next hurdle was my wife's postsecondary degree certificate from a university in Bangalore. We were called by their office and told that the certificate was ready and could be picked up. We drove to the university and were made to wait for several hours and finally told by the clerk that the degree appeared to be misplaced. We knew they wanted us to grease some palms, but we had decided against this. We barged our way into the vice-chancellor's office and expressed our frustration in no uncertain terms. The officer was taken aback by our boldness and asked us to wait outside his office. Within no time, the same clerk who said that the degree was misplaced came out and handed it over to us. The whole process from the time we applied for immigration to Canada to receiving the visas took just about nine months. So God kept His promise of opening up the windows of heaven by bringing us to Canada with His uplifted right hand, and then He poured out the greatest blessing for us that we had no more room to receive it by completely healing our daughter of asthma! Glory to God in the highest! God forbid, if you have ever held your little child in your arms gasping for the breath of life, then you will understand what this meant for us. This is the mighty God whom we serve!

"I will sing to the Lord as long as I live; I will sing praise to my God while I have any being" (Psalm 104:33 AMPC).

Faith Is an Act

"Now FAITH is the assurance (the confirmation, the title deed) of the things [we] hope for, being the proof of things [we] do not see and the conviction of their reality [faith perceiving as real fact what is not revealed to the senses]" (Hebrews 11:1 AMPC).

This verse clearly tells us that faith is "now"—that is it's in the present tense. So if you are releasing your faith for something that you are hoping for, then it is done there and then though you don't see it in the natural yet as is clear from the later part of the verse. Secondly, faith is the title deed or evidence of the things hoped for. In a court of law, the judge investigates an "act" that was committed based on the evidence presented, as he was not present physically at the scene of the "act" to see it with his own eyes. The evidence presented proves that the act was committed. So when you release your faith for something you are hoping for in the natural, then the act has taken place in the spiritual realm, and it leaves evidence (the tangible substance of faith that you can feel in your spirit) that the act is already committed, though you don't yet see or feel it manifest in the natural. However, the evidence is proof enough for the judge to give the verdict that the act was committed. Now you can move ahead to take the necessary actions concerning the thing that you released your faith for. But here is the catch! If you do not take action believing that it's done, then the thing you were hoping for remains a hope and never manifests. It's like having the cashier's cheque in your hand but unless you go and cash it in the bank, it remains a piece of paper in your hand and never turns into hard cash that can be used.

Look at the instances when people received healing from Jesus. When they acted in faith either before Jesus did anything or after He did or said something, they received that which they were hoping for or needed. The woman with the bleeding issue acted in faith by going and touching the clothes of Jesus from behind in the crowd.

"Jesus turned around and, seeing her, He said, Take courage, daughter! Your faith has made you well. And at once the woman was restored to health" (Matthew 9:22 AMPC).

The blind beggar Bartimaeus, when he heard the crowd and realized that Jesus was passing by, began shouting and begging Jesus to have mercy on him. Now look at his action when Jesus called him:

> And Jesus stopped and said, Call him. And they called the blind man, telling him, Take courage! Get up! He is calling you.
> *And throwing off his outer garment, he leaped up and came to Jesus.*
> And Jesus said to him, What do you want Me to do for you? And the blind man said to Him, Master, let me receive my sight.
> And Jesus said to him, Go your way; *your faith has healed you. And at once he received his sight* and accompanied Jesus on the road. (Mark 10:49–52 AMPC)

Now, a few cases where people were told to act before they got their healing. The man with the withered hand acted on Jesus's command:

> And it occurred on another Sabbath that when He went into the synagogue and taught, a man was present whose right hand was withered.
> Then He glanced around at them all and said to the man, *Stretch out your hand! And he did so, and his hand was fully restored like the other one.* (Luke 6:6, 10 AMPC)

Jesus healed a man blind from his birth by asking him to do something:

> As HE passed along, He noticed a man blind from his birth.... He spat on the ground and made clay (mud) with His saliva, and He spread it [as ointment] on the man's eyes. And He said to him, *Go, wash in the Pool of Siloam*—which means Sent. *So he went and washed, and came back seeing.* (John 9:1–7 AMPC)

The man did not receive sight in this case till he obeyed and acted on what was asked of him to do. If the man had doubted and not gone or if he would have washed with water from some other place or just wiped out his eyes he would not have received his sight. Here's a passage that proves that doubt hinders or stops the miracle:

> And in the fourth watch [between 3:00–6:00 a.m.] of the night, Jesus came to them, walking on the sea.
> And when the disciples saw Him walking on the sea, they were terrified and said, It is a ghost! And they screamed out with fright.
> But instantly He spoke to them, saying, Take courage! I AM! Stop being afraid!
> And Peter answered Him, Lord, if it is You, command me to come to You on the water.
> He said, Come! *So Peter got out of the boat and walked on the water*, and he came toward Jesus.
> *But when he perceived and felt the strong wind, he was frightened, and as he began to sink, he cried out, Lord, save me [from death]!*
> Instantly Jesus reached out His hand and caught and held him, saying to him, *O you of little faith, why did you doubt?* (Matthew 14:25–31 AMPC)

Peter started in faith to defy the laws of physics, but the moment he doubted, physical laws overpowered spiritual laws!

I will go back to the story of my company, Fahrenheit Communications, to highlight this principle of faith in action and doubt being the killer of the miracle. From the time we applied for Canadian immigration, I started to think about what would need to be done about the company, which, at that point, employed about ten people, and we had just moved into a brand-new office that I had furnished beautifully in International Tech Park Bangalore (ITPB), which was a dream destination for me to have the office in. ITPB was mooted in 1992 by the then prime ministers of India and Singapore, PV Narasimha Rao and Goh Chok Tong, respectively, to replicate Singapore's quality infrastructure in India.

I did not want to shut down the company and take away the employment from my team members, whom I valued and considered as my family. So I researched the possibility of selling it to another company that would keep my people employed and also put a good value on something I had built over nine years with a lot of love and passion. Some people I talked to in the advertising world discouraged me saying, "Yours is a very small company and you being the face of the company, leaving would mean losing all clients." So no one would be interested in buying desks, chairs, and some computers with the liability of paying salaries to the people.

One day, I was standing at a scrap shop near my home, and God said to me, "If scrap can sell, then surely your profit-making company would sell." At that time, my company was doing a business of about $160,000 annually. I moved in faith and hired a business consultant to work on the valuation of the company and find a buyer.

Time passed quickly, and we had our immigration visas in hand within nine months. The consultant could not find any buyer in India but was in talks with a company in Dubai. As we were nearing the date when we needed to fly to Canada, I was getting worried about the future of the company, its employees, and its clients. So I moved out of faith in the word that God had spoken to me at the scrap shop nine months back and went ahead to convert the company into a partnership concern, joining hands with a young person who was willing to come in as a partner and run the show. This was where I blew my miracle! Fear and doubt are the enemies of faith.

On the weekend before we were going to fly to Canada, my business consultant brought in the head of this advertising firm in Dubai to meet me at my office. He offered me $250,000 for the company and went on to say that he could even arrange for the money to be put in a bank in Canada or given in cash once we landed in Canada. I discussed this with my partner and offered to give him his share as per his partnership percentage in the company. But this young man wanted to run the company and did not want it to be sold. My wife and I discussed it overnight and decided to decline the buyout deal so that this young man and his sweet family would not be hurt after we left the country.

Faith Needs to Be Qualified

Not just that every religion talks about faith, but even the atheists and agnostics do things or act in faith. Their faith can be in false gods; created things (sun, moon, stars, animals, or carved images); technology; science; or worse in themselves as the be-all and end-all. This kind of faith is delusional as the thing in which faith is expressed is itself not stable and can change with time or circumstances not to mention that the thing itself may be lifeless. Such faith will eventually fail and destroy the beholder.

Let's look at what the Bible says about faith: "So faith comes by hearing [what is told], and what is heard comes by the preaching [of the message that came from the lips] of Christ (the Messiah Himself)" (Romans 10:17 AMPC).

So faith comes by hearing and hearing about the message of Jesus Christ. Why should faith in Jesus Christ be the only true faith that gives abundant life here on earth and life eternal (salvation)? Because Jesus is the beginning of all things in God:

> IN THE beginning [before all time] was the Word (Christ), and the Word was with God, and the Word was God Himself.

He was present originally with God.

All things were made and came into existence through Him; and without Him was not even one thing made that has come into being.

In Him was Life, and the Life was the Light of men. (John 1:1–4 AMPC)

Someone may say that you are quoting from the Bible and saying that it is the truth, but I have my own religious books that I believe hold the truth. Well then, have the courage and audacity to read your religious books and also the Bible with an open mind and pure heart to find the truth. Because there can only be one true God just like we can have only one true natural father whose sperm fertilizes the mother's egg.

Has anyone in the history of mankind made these claims about himself and left historical proofs to verify the authenticity of these claims?

"And God said to Moses, I AM WHO I AM and WHAT I AM, and I WILL BE WHAT I WILL BE; and He said, You shall say this to the Israelites: I AM has sent me to you!" (Exodus 3:14 AMPC).

When God calls Himself the "I Am" in Exodus 3, it's a pivotal moment in redemptive history. God reveals Himself to His people and comes to redeem them out of exile and lead them into a new life. God's name discloses who He is and what He is like. He is the I Am, the eternal, unchanging, self-existent one, infinite and glorious in every way, and above and beyond all created things. He is God.

"Jesus replied, 'I assure you, most solemnly I tell you, before Abraham was born, I AM'" (John 8:58 AMPC).

When Jesus applies the title "I Am" to Himself, He claims to be God (John 8:58). Not a helper to God or a great teacher, but the divine, eternal, preexistent, infinite, perfect Being. He is Israel's God. He is greater than Moses because he is the God of Moses. He has life in Himself, and He can give life to us. The Jews knew that taking on this title was making such a claim, which is why they immediately picked up stones to kill Him (John 8:59).

The seven "I Am" statements in John might best be understood as falling under and echoing this initial, ultimate claim of Jesus. He is God, and He is the God of Israel. All the Old Testament and God's redemptive acts were pointing to the coming of Jesus as the God-in-flesh and the fulfillment of all the Old Testament types and shadows.[2]

1) "I Am the Bread of Life"

> Jesus replied, "*I am the Bread of Life*. He who comes to Me will never be hungry, and he who believes in and cleaves to and trusts in and relies on Me will never thirst anymore [at any time]." (John 6:35 AMPC)

2) "I Am the Light of the World"

> Once more Jesus addressed the crowd. He said, "*I am the Light of the world*. He who follows Me will not be walking in the dark but will have the Light which is Life." (John 8:12 AMPC)

3) "I Am the Door or Gate"
4) "I Am the Good Shepherd"

> So Jesus said again, I assure you, most solemnly I tell you, that *I Myself am the Door for the sheep*.
> All others who came [as such] before Me are thieves and robbers, but the [true] sheep did not listen to and obey them.
> *I am the Door; anyone who enters in through Me will be saved (will live)*. He will come in and he will go out [freely], and will find pasture.

---

[2] https://indycrowe.com/2019/02/13/the-7-i-am-statements-of-jesus-ot-background-nt-meaning/

The thief comes only in order to steal and kill and destroy. I came that they may have and enjoy life, and have it in abundance (to the full, till it overflows).

I am the Good Shepherd. The Good Shepherd risks and lays down His [own] life for the sheep. (John 10:7–11 AMPC)

5) "I Am the Resurrection and the Life"

Jesus said to her, *I am [Myself] the Resurrection and the Life.* Whoever believes in (adheres to, trusts in, and relies on) Me, although he may die, yet he shall live;

And whoever continues to live and believes in (has faith in, cleaves to, and relies on) Me shall never [actually] die at all. Do you believe this? (John 11:25–26 AMPC)

6) "I Am the Way, the Truth, and the Life"

Jesus said to him, "*I am the Way and the Truth and the Life; no one comes to the Father except by (through) Me.*" (John 14:6 AMPC)

7) "I Am the True Vine"

I AM the True Vine, and My Father is the Vinedresser.

Any branch in Me that does not bear fruit [that stops bearing] He cuts away (trims off, takes away); and He cleanses and repeatedly prunes every branch that continues to bear fruit, to make it bear more and richer and more excellent fruit.

> You are cleansed and pruned already, because of the word which I have given you [the teachings I have discussed with you].
>
> *Dwell in Me, and I will dwell in you.* [Live in Me, and I will live in you.] Just as no branch can bear fruit of itself without abiding in (being vitally united to) the vine, neither can you bear fruit unless you abide in Me.
>
> *I am the Vine; you are the branches.* Whoever lives in Me and I in him bears much (abundant) fruit. However, apart from Me [cut off from vital union with Me] you can do nothing.
>
> If a person does not dwell in Me, he is thrown out like a [broken-off] branch, and withers; such branches are gathered up and thrown into the fire, and they are burned.
>
> *If you live in Me [abide vitally united to Me] and My words remain in you* and continue to live in your hearts, *ask whatever you will, and it shall be done for you.* (John 15:1–7 AMPC)

Now, this faith in the person of Jesus Christ is the true faith that can do wonders and miracles while you are on earth as per His promise in John 15:7: "*Ask whatever you will, and it shall be done for you.*"

Faith Is a Muscle

All of us have muscles in our bodies, but not all can lift weights like Arnold Schwarzenegger because he has developed his muscles over a period of time with intense exercising. Similarly, we can use our faith to the measure we build it up by continuously exercising it in our day-to-day living. We exercise our faith in the car we drive or the airplane we travel in to take us safely to the destination without breaking down or crashing while at 120 kph or thirty thousand feet above ground. Then why should we not exercise our faith in the wonderful, counselor, mighty God, everlasting Father, Prince of peace, Jesus Christ (Isaiah 9:6) to get us the things we want in life that we hope for whether it's our health, wealth, relationships, or just the little things to get us by the day?

We came to Canada in 2015 as a family leaving behind a well-established business, debt-free house, family, and friends with faith in a good God. There were more than fifteen loving people from our church family to see us off in India, and we landed in Toronto to go to a hotel with no one to receive us and with just enough money to keep us going for six months. But we brought with us our faith in the God who never fails us. Our first home in Canada was a brand-new townhome that we rented not a basement. The first job I got after five months was with a salary of $90,000, and within exactly two years, we bought our first house in Canada. We were far off from the stories we had heard of the struggles that new immigrants go through. Faith will stretch you, but the more you exercise it in the living God, the stronger it will get.

"For this very reason, adding your diligence [to the divine promises], *employ every effort in exercising your faith* to develop virtue (excellence, resolution, Christian energy), and in [exercising] virtue [develop] knowledge (intelligence)" (2 Peter 1:5 AMPC).

Faith Is a Fight

The devil knows that your most holy faith is the biggest asset you can have to flow in the power of God, and he will not leave any opportunity throughout your life to steal your faith.

> Be well balanced (temperate, sober of mind), be vigilant and cautious at all times; for that enemy of yours, the devil, roams around like a lion roaring [in fierce hunger], seeking someone to seize upon and devour.
>
> Withstand him; *be firm in faith [against his onset—rooted, established, strong, immovable, and determined]*, knowing that the same (identical) sufferings are appointed to your brotherhood

(the whole body of Christians) throughout the world. (1 Peter 5:8–9 AMPC)

Every promise of God in the Bible is for us to live abundantly in every area of life on earth and thereafter to enter eternal life with God (salvation). But we have to take these promises by faith and even be saved through our faith.

> But without faith, it is impossible to please and be satisfactory to Him. For whoever would come near to God must [necessarily] believe that God exists and that He is the rewarder of those who earnestly and diligently seek Him [out]. (Hebrews 11:6 AMPC)

> For it is by free grace (God's unmerited favor) that you are saved (delivered from judgment and made partakers of Christ's salvation) *through [your] faith*. And this [salvation] is not of yourselves [of your own doing, it came not through your own striving], but it is the gift of God. (Ephesians 2:8 AMPC)

But we who believe are not left without help because the Bible says,

> And after you have suffered a little while, the God of all grace [Who imparts all blessing and favor], Who has called you to His [own] eternal glory in Christ Jesus, will Himself complete and make you what you ought to be, establish and ground you securely, and strengthen, and settle you. (1 Peter 5:10 AMPC)

Even as I write this book, we as a family are undergoing the worst attack in our lives and our hearts are bleeding. Many times

I went into phases of depression, cried, stopped writing, and even doubted my faith. Sure enough, the devil didn't want this book to come out, for this would be the best I have ever done in my life to serve God, even better and more satisfying than the company that I started and built back in India. This is the story of my life poured out as a fragrant offering unto God.

But the Lord is always at hand to help those who will not give up and fight the good fight of faith.

"Fight the good fight of the faith; lay hold of the eternal life to which you were summoned and [for which] you confessed the good confession [of faith] before many witnesses" (1 Timothy 6:12 AMPC).

Love Walk

"For God so greatly loved and dearly prized the world that He [even] gave up His only begotten (unique) Son, so that whoever believes in (trusts in, clings to, relies on) Him shall not perish (come to destruction, be lost) but have eternal (everlasting) life" (John 3:16 AMPC).

All this while we have read about what a believer needs to do to walk in the promises of God and His divine power. But our love walk is a response and natural outcome of the greatest love that humanity has ever experienced or will ever experience. This is what differentiates Christianity from all the other faiths of the world. Every other religion is man's pursuit of God to appease and somehow achieve salvation but Christianity is God's pursuit of man to make him righteous (right standing with Him) by the sending of His Son, Jesus Christ, into the world as a human, born of a virgin, to take on Himself the sins of all humanity and by pouring of His sinless blood be the atoning sacrifice for the salvation of everyone who will believe in Him.

"In this is love: not that we loved God, but that He loved us and sent His Son to be the propitiation (the atoning sacrifice) for our sins" (1 John 4:10 AMPC).

God knew that it was impossible for man to ever be completely devoid of sin and be able to get right with Him by their own efforts.

> As it is written, None is righteous, just and truthful and upright and conscientious, no, not one. (Romans 3:10 AMPC)

> Since all have sinned and are falling short of the honor and glory which God bestows and receives. (Romans 3:23 AMPC)

So He planned it even before the creation of the world, to send His Son at the appointed time to die for our sins and be raised again to life so we may have life everlasting with Him.

"Even as [in His love] He chose us [picked us out for Himself as His own] in Christ before the foundation of the world, that we should be holy (consecrated and set apart for Him) and blameless in His sight, even above reproach, before Him in love" (Ephesians 1:4 AMPC).

Agnostics and skeptics have put forward this question: Why did the all-knowing God who knew everything from the beginning to the end ever create man if He knew in His foresight that man would sin and then God would have to send His only Son to redeem man from the fall?

The answer to this question can be found by analyzing the nature of God and His creation, which is man. Firstly, the Bible says that God is love.

"He who does not love has not become acquainted with God [does not and never did know Him], for God is love." (1 John 4:8 AMPC).

Secondly, God created man in His likeness.

"So God created man in His own image, in the image and likeness of God He created him; male and female He created them" (Genesis 1:27 AMPC).

The world is filled with books, movies, and stories (personal or someone we know) of how people get treated by their children most of the time once they get old. Some stories are horrific and others not so dramatic, but there is always an element of truth about the love of children growing cold toward their parents. If you search your heart honestly, then you will know that this is true to some degree to what you have done in thought or deed toward your old parents or your grown-up children have done to you.

So if the man who has the likeness of God goes on to have children knowing the pains of bringing up a child and the eventual heartbreaks he will have to go through at the hand of his very own child, then why is God questioned about His nature of love that led Him to create mankind?

Once this is established, then the next question props up in the mind of the skeptic. Why did God create sin or the devil who leads man to sin? The answer to that question is that God did not create sin. Sin was the result of free will that led Lucifer to choose to think that he could ascend higher than God (*Revelations 12:9*), and with the same free will, man chose to disobey God when he ate the forbidden fruit in the Garden of Eden (Genesis 2, 3).

Then the skeptic may ask, "Why did God give free will to Lucifer and man?" The answer to that is simple. God did not want a bunch of robots around Himself and, Mr. Skeptic, you can now circle back to the love nature of God to know why He did not want to create robots and why God even created anything that exists. These basic questions need clarity and answers as many people, especially the young growing up in current times can stumble and then their whole faith gets shipwrecked. Actually, I will not be too off to say that 95 percent of Christians are skeptics as they believe some of the Bible and reject or doubt some parts that do not conform to their way of thinking or comfort zone. Someone has rightly called these Christians "unbelieving believers"!

Now that we have established the existence of a loving God who loved us first, how do we respond to this unconditional love? Jesus provides the answer in these verses:

> Teacher, which kind of commandment is great and important (the principal kind) in the Law? [Some commandments are light—which are heavy?]
>
> And He replied to him, *You shall love the Lord your God with all your heart and with all your soul and with all your mind (intellect).*

> This is the great (most important, principal) and first commandment.
> And a second is like it: *You shall love your neighbor as [you do] yourself.*
> These two commandments sum up and upon them depend all the Law and the Prophets. (Matthew 22:36–40 AMPC)

If we can sincerely rearrange our lives with respect to these things that we read earlier in the book, then I believe we can with a good measure of confidence say that we love God.

- Believe in the one and only true God.
- Discipline our lives according to the Word of God.
- Be obedient to God.
- Read and meditate on the Word.
- Act in faith.
- Walk in love with others.
- Develop a consistent prayer life.

And if we start doing these, then loving our neighbor (spouse, family, friends, brothers, and sisters in the body of Christ and unknown people) will be an easy outcome. There are other commands that Jesus gave on the love walk that can be found in the Bible, and as we grow in our walk with God, we will get skillful in them with the help of the Holy Spirit. The ultimate goal is to be able to love like Jesus loved when He forgave even the ones who crucified Him.

> And when they came to the place which is called The Skull [Latin: Calvary; Hebrew: Golgotha], there they crucified Him, and [along with] the criminals, one on the right and one on the left.
> And *Jesus prayed, Father, forgive them, for they know not what they do.* And they divided His

garments and distributed them by casting lots for them. (Luke 23:33–34 AMPC)

Easier said than done? Yes. But try practicing forgiveness, and you will realize that forgiving the one who hurt you and doing good to them instead will actually do more good to yourself.

Let me come back to my story of blowing up the miracle of the sale of my company in mid-2015 when we moved to Canada. The young man who partnered with me started running the company, and within a few months of our settling in Canada, he wanted to buy out my controlling stake in the company with a paltry amount compared to what the Dubai-based company had put the valuation at and said that the payout would be over a period of time through the profit the company makes. This hurt me deeply as we had let go of the buyout offer of $250,000 in favor of this person's desire to run the company. I took offense and got very upset, and the result was an exchange of hurtful words between us. I cracked open the door to the devil by my wrong attitude and behavior. God disciplined me by allowing the devil to take away the job that I was blessed with here in Canada.

"Know also in your [minds and] hearts that, as a man disciplines and instructs his son, so the Lord your God disciplines and instructs you" (Deuteronomy 8:5 AMPC).

I repented to God and forgave this young man, who I felt had stabbed in my back and we agreed to part ways. As a born-again believer, you must know that the moment you repent of a sin truly in your heart, the good God forgives you instantly out of His loving nature.

"For if you forgive people their trespasses [their reckless and willful sins, leaving them, letting them go, and giving up resentment], your heavenly Father will also forgive you" (Matthew 6:14 AMPC).

Following this, I went to India to sell my property, met this young man, and hugged him lovingly. I sold the company to a friend of mine for a very small amount, which was enough to recover the investment I had made in the new office infrastructure before moving to Canada. I took this painful loss to the Lord in prayer believing in my heart that my inheritance will come from Him one day. My biological dad had not left a penny for me as inheritance, but the void of a responsible earthly father was filled in my life by God, and I looked up to Him for my inheritance.

"Knowing [with all certainty] that it is from the Lord [and not from men] that you will receive the inheritance which is your [real] reward. [The One Whom] you are actually serving [is] the Lord Christ (the Messiah)" (Colossians 3:24 AMPC).

Love walk is the most important thing that we will have to keep reminding ourselves of, as we start experiencing the power of God in our lives for the Bible says, "IF I [can] speak in the tongues of men and [even] of angels, but have not love (that reasoning, intentional, spiritual devotion such as is inspired by God's love for and in us), I am only a noisy gong or a clanging cymbal" (1 Corinthians 13:1 AMPC).

The human heart can get proud very easily with power, and here we are talking of divine power which is limitless. We will need to guard our hearts carefully and continuously as we start using God's power to help ourselves and others.

"Pride goes before destruction and a haughty spirit before a fall" (Proverbs 16:18 AMPC).

Prayer Life

Prayer is a word that is grossly misunderstood and loosely used not just by unbelievers but even Christians. I have heard well-meaning Christians say during any crisis: "Now all we can do is pray" or "Nothing can be done now except prayer." If you go to prayer with that attitude and mindset then the battle is already lost.

On the other hand people from all walks of faith say, "There is power in prayer." This statement is true and like saying there is power in nuclear fusion or fission. This power can be used to do good (create electricity) or bring about destruction (bombs). The god of this world (the devil) has powers that he makes available to anyone who worships him.

> For we are not wrestling with flesh and blood [contending only with physical opponents], but against the despotisms, against the powers, against [the master spirits who are] the world rulers of this present darkness, against the spirit forces of wickedness in the heavenly (supernatural) sphere. (Ephesians 6:12 AMPC)

The devil has the power to get you the things of the world for temporary enjoyment like money, fame, success, or even health by stopping the progression of sickness and disease or not inflicting it on you (Matthew 4:8–9, 1 Peter 5:8) to deceive you into worshiping him but his eventual goal is to kill, steal, and destroy. Jesus said, "The thief (devil) comes only in order to steal and kill and destroy. I came that they may have and enjoy life, and have it in abundance (to the full, till it overflows)" (John 10:10 AMPC).

"For the god of this world has blinded the unbelievers' minds [that they should not discern the truth], preventing them from seeing the illuminating light of the Gospel of the glory of Christ (the Messiah), Who is the Image and Likeness of God" (2 Corinthians 4:4 AMPC).

Now let's look at how Jesus taught us to pray and get hold of the authority of the believer.

> Pray, therefore, like this: Our Father Who is in heaven, hallowed (kept holy) be Your name.
> Your kingdom come, Your will be done on earth as it is in heaven.
> Give us this day our daily bread.
> And forgive us our debts, as we also have forgiven (left, remitted, and let go of the debts, and have given up resentment against) our debtors.
> And lead (bring) us not into temptation, but deliver us from the evil one. For Yours is the kingdom and the power and the glory forever. Amen. (Matthew 6:9–13 AMPC)

Notice that Jesus said, "Your kingdom come, Your will be done on earth as it is in heaven." That makes it clear that God's kingdom is in heaven, and the hearts of the believers but not the rest of this world (everything on earth, its atmosphere, and the nonbelievers). Jesus asks the believers to pray to God for His will to be done on earth as it is in heaven. So unless the believers pray, God is limited to doing anything on earth as He cannot go against His own principles that He set in motion by His words. This biblical truth has evaded the understanding of most Christians. As we read earlier, when Jesus ascended to heaven after His resurrection, He gave *all authority* in heaven and on earth to not just the eleven disciples but every disciple of His till the end of this age (Church Age).

> Jesus approached and, breaking the silence, said to them, *All authority (all power of rule) in heaven and on earth has been given to Me.*
>
> *Go then* and make disciples of all the nations, baptizing them into the name of the Father and of the Son and of the Holy Spirit,
>
> Teaching them to observe everything that I have commanded you, *and behold, I am with you all the days (perpetually, uniformly, and on every occasion), to the [very] close and consummation of the age.* Amen (so let it be). (Matthew 28:18–20 AMPC)

The legal system of democracy gives the power to administer justice to the Supreme Court and execution powers to the police. The policeman uses that authority to bring law and order to society, not the judge. The traffic stops when a policeman stands on the road and just gestures with his hands because of the authority given to him. If a judge stands with his judicial robe in the middle of the road, then at best, he will get some smiles or curious looks. But when the judge enters the courtroom, then everyone stands.

Similarly, when Jesus gave all authority to the Church in the current dispensation of time (Church Age), then He could not go against His own system that He put in place. Jesus expects the Church to exert that authority in His name to bring about the plans and purposes of God on earth and in the heavens (not the highest heaven). We execute that authority by all kinds of prayers in the name of Jesus and by our words spoken in His name. I have heard skeptics say that if believers have to do everything and God cannot do anything in the current dispensation (Church Age), then what is He doing, and what's the point of Him being there? Well, God is waiting for believers to truly believe in Jesus and ask His help for the impossible things that man cannot do. On the flip side, if God would do everything and not need a man to participate, then man would throw up his hands in despair, saying, "What's the point of life if all my doing is meaningless or not needed?" You can never satisfy a skeptic.

Now let's take hold of what this power and authority means that Jesus gave to you and me who believe in Him:

> And [so that you can know and understand] what is the *immeasurable* and *unlimited* and *surpassing greatness* of *His power in and for us who believe*, as demonstrated in the working of His mighty strength,
> Which He exerted in Christ when He raised Him from the dead and seated Him at His [own] right hand in the heavenly [places],
> Far above all rule and authority and power and dominion and every name that is named [above every title that can be conferred], not only in this age and in this world, but also in the age and the world which are to come.
> And He has put all things under His feet and has appointed Him the universal and supreme *Head of the church* [a headship exercised throughout the church],
> *Which is His body*, the fullness of Him Who fills all in all [for in that body lives the full measure of Him Who makes everything complete, and Who fills everything everywhere with Himself]. (Ephesians 1:19–23 AMPC)

The power is not in the believer himself, but it's in the Name of the One who has given it to the believer. Just like the policeman does not have any power in himself when he stands in a civilian dress, but the moment he wears the uniform given to him, then he can use the power.

The believer can use this power only within the boundaries and purposes of God. Just like the policeman who stands to lose his job if he goes out of his boundary of authority or misuses the power, the believer's authority has its boundaries that if he crosses can be detrimental.

"You shall not take the name of the Lord your God in vain, for the Lord will not hold him guiltless who takes His name in falsehood or without purpose" (Deuteronomy 5:11 AMPC).

You can use this God-given power for yourself to get help in times of trouble, but you will be given more power when you become a conduit of this power for the benefit of other people.

While I was in college pursuing my bachelor's degree in pharmaceutical sciences, I got involved with a bunch of rowdy students. The main guy in this group was a tough-looking goon, and I got pulled to him because of his personality. One night before leaving the city for summer vacation to go home, we were drinking till past midnight. I had opened the door wide open for the devil to destroy my life. After getting drunk, this chap and I wanted to go out on his bike for a ride. Coming out of his house, we saw a few people going about making a lot of noise. This boy started yelling at them in his drunken state and picked up a fistfight with them, and I got involved too. We beat these people up so badly that one of them, an old man, got seriously hurt and fell. So we quickly drove away from the scene on the bike.

The next day, I traveled to a city called Kochi where my mother lived at that time. After some days, I got a call from this goon saying that the old man we had beaten was in critical condition in hospital, and somehow, these people got to know the college I was in and may report the incident to the college and the police. He started blackmailing me saying that I should send him money to bribe the people we had fought with. This put so much fear in me that I didn't even want to go back to college. But I had still not repented to God. Then one day, we were again drinking in a bar with my cousins, and as we came out, we picked a fight with a group of boys. I fractured my right thumb after punching one of them. The next morning, I came to my senses and repented profusely, asking God to forgive me and remove this goon from my life with whom I had got involved in college.

The vacation was over, and it was time to head back to college, but the fear of meeting this goon in college and the repercussions of my actions kept looming large. But God had already heard my prayer of repentance and help was on the way; the angel of the Lord was set in motion. I went back to college, and a friend of mine brought me the news that this goon was killed in a road accident while I was on vacation. It may sound cruel, but I was so happy and relieved to hear this news. I am not suggesting that God removed him from the face of the earth but am not ruling out the possibility also. Whatever happened I was rescued by God.

There is brute power in earnest prayers to the living God. Look how David prayed regarding his enemies:

> Contend, O Lord, with those who contend with me; fight against those who fight against me!
> Take hold of shield and buckler, and stand up for my help!
> Draw out also the spear and javelin and close up the way of those who pursue and persecute me. Say to me, I am your deliverance!
> Let them be put to shame and dishonor who seek and require my life; let them be turned back and confounded who plan my hurt!
> Let them be as chaff before the wind, with the Angel of the Lord driving them on!
> Let their way be through dark and slippery places, with the Angel of the Lord pursuing and afflicting them. (Psalm 35:1–6 AMPC)

There are a variety of prayers mentioned in the Bible, but we will not get into that except a small note on the most powerful form of prayer that is available to believers about which the world has no idea about and a very tiny percentage of Christians have taken hold of it.

Prayer in Tongues

The gift of tongues was given by Jesus to believers when He ascended to heaven and sent the Holy Spirit to live inside of born-again believers.

"And they were all filled (diffused throughout their souls) with the Holy Spirit and began to speak in other (different, foreign) languages (tongues), as the Spirit kept giving them clear and loud expression [in each tongue in appropriate words]" (Acts 2:4 AMPC).

This gift is given to believers to talk to God. It bypasses the mind because the mind does not understand it and goes unto God directly unhindered by the devil as even he does not understand it.

"For one who speaks in an [unknown] tongue speaks not to men but to God, for no one understands or catches his meaning because in the [Holy] Spirit he utters secret truths and hidden things [not obvious to the understanding]" (1 Corinthians 14:2 AMPC).

This is the most powerful way to pray as it gets the perfect will of God done on earth because now you are not praying with the limited understanding of your mind but with the infinite mind of God. The Holy Spirit searches the deep things of God and gives those to the believer to pray out.

"Yet to us God has unveiled and revealed them by and through His Spirit, for the [Holy] Spirit searches diligently, exploring and examining everything, even sounding the profound and bottomless things of God [the divine counsels and things hidden and beyond man's scrutiny]" (1 Corinthians 2:10 AMPC).

Since this form of prayer is so powerful, your mind and soul influenced by the devil will fight against it by telling you that this is not making sense, or it is a waste of time, or it feels weird. See, the devil recognizes that when you start praying in tongues, then you become invincible as he is not able to decipher what you are saying so he cannot hinder or delay the answer to what you have prayed out (Daniel 10:12–13 AMPC).

I started the year 2024 by praying in tongues at 12:00 a.m. on January 1 and went on till 5:00 a.m. at a stretch. This was the first time in my life I had prayed for that long and at the fifth hour, the power of God filled me like a gusher. I could not contain that awesome power in my body and started begging God to let it flow out of my body to heal anyone who needed healing.

I am not a writer by any stretch of imagination, and this is my first book. But I could write 90 percent of this book over a period of two weeks as I was praying in tongues over long hours at night. That's the power of praying in tongues.

Authority of Believers to Lead Abundant Lives

Before we get into understanding how to flow in the authority as believers in Jesus Christ, we must be clear on how we as human beings are formed, as every part of our being will come into play in the process.

God created humans from the dust of the earth into a body, soul, and spirit being in His likeness (quality).

> God said, Let Us [Father, Son, and Holy Spirit] make mankind in Our image, after Our likeness, and let them have complete authority over the fish of the sea, the birds of the air, the [tame] beasts, and over all of the earth, and over everything that creeps upon the earth.
>
> So God created man in His own image, in the image and likeness of God He created him; male and female He created them. (Genesis 1:26–27 AMPC)

Some people think soul and spirit are the same thing, but the Bible is clear on the distinction between the two.

> And may the God of peace Himself sanctify you through and through [separate you from profane things, make you pure and wholly consecrated

to God]; and may your *spirit* and *soul* and *body* be preserved sound and complete [and found] blameless at the coming of our Lord Jesus Christ (the Messiah). (1 Thessalonians 5:23 AMPC)

Our spirit is what makes us different from animals because God breathed the spirit into our bodies, and the spirit gives us the ability to form words (speech) and have a meaningful conversation.

"Then the Lord God formed man from the dust of the ground and breathed into his nostrils the breath or spirit of life, and man became a living being" (Genesis 2:7 AMPC).

The world recognizes the human spirit in terms like conscience, instinct, gut feeling, hunch, impulse, inclination, intuition, or savvy sense.

Our soul is a combination of mind (intellect), emotions (feelings), and will (choice). Almost all the battles in our lives are either won or lost in this area of our being.

Our body is the perishable covering of our soul and spirit.

Jesus came to make our spirit alive unto God (born again) and save our soul, that both of these may go to heaven taking on new spiritual bodies once the earthly body perishes (death) or is transformed (raptured if we are still alive when Jesus comes back) (1 Corinthians 15:50–53 AMPC).

So the moment we accept Jesus into our lives as Lord and Savior, our spirit becomes alive unto God and gets sealed by the sinless blood of Jesus Christ that He poured on the cross and the devil cannot touch our spirit any longer. From this moment forward, we keep working on our soul and body to keep them aligned to the perfect will of God so that we may live abundant lives in the power of God.

The devil, who is a defeated foe, keeps on trying to devour these two areas (soul and body) of born-again believers' lives as he does not want them to avail of all the blessings of God in their lives here on earth as he knows that now he can do nothing to prevent them from going to heaven.

But we will be victorious every time the devil attacks us because of this promise of God: "Little children, you are of God [you belong to Him] and have [already] defeated and overcome them [the agents of the antichrist], because He Who lives in you is greater (mightier) than he who is in the world" (1 John 4:4 AMPC).

The three most important areas of our lives where we need the power of God to help us lead abundant lives that Jesus promised are health, wealth, and peace.

Believer's Authority over Health

We all struggle with health issues throughout our lives and thank God for medical professionals and healthcare institutions that we can avail of. In addition to these, believers have divine help available which they can tap into by using the authority given by God in the name of Jesus Christ. We can use this divine power for ourselves and others.

> Confess to one another therefore your faults (your slips, your false steps, your offenses, your sins) and pray [also] for one another, that you may be *healed and restored* [to a spiritual tone of mind and heart]. The earnest (heartfelt, continued) prayer of a righteous man makes tremendous power available [dynamic in its working]. (James 5:16 AMPC)

When God created the universe, He put in motion these laws to help human beings remain in good health throughout their lives as He knew that man would sin and that would lead him to sickness, decay, and death. He made the *natural elements* (the smallest discovered to date has been named by physicists as "quarks," which are subatomic particles and considered the building blocks of the universe[3]) from which all medicines and medical devices are made. Then God

---

[3] https://www.sciencedaily.com/releases/2019/03/190304121449.htm

made human beings in *His likeness* (giving them the mind of God to discover, innovate, and learn medicine and the practice of medicine) and finally, the most powerful ingredient to get health when human discoveries, innovations, and education fail—*His name (Jesus Christ)* and the authority to use His name to overcome all sickness and disease by faith.

> [When] a certain man crippled from his birth was being carried along, who was laid each day at that gate of the temple [which is] called Beautiful, so that he might beg for charitable gifts from those who entered the temple.
> So when he saw Peter and John about to go into the temple, he asked them to give him a gift.
> And Peter directed his gaze intently at him, and so did John, and said, Look at us!
> And [the man] paid attention to them, expecting that he was going to get something from them.
> But Peter said, Silver and gold (money) I do not have; but what I do have, that I give to you: *in [the use of] the name of Jesus Christ of Nazareth, walk!*
> Then he took hold of the man's right hand with a firm grip and raised him up. And at once his feet and ankle bones became strong and steady. (Acts 3:2–7 AMPC)

From ages past, human beings have learned from nature and taken up the elements thereof to develop medicine. Even the practice of medicine is a learned behavior that uses the principles of divine healing to diagnose and treat ailments in the human body.

Let's see how the divine healer, Jesus Christ, demonstrated medicine and the practice of medicine while He walked on earth and gave this authority to believers before ascending to heaven.

Jesus demonstrated the use of medicine and divine healing.

As HE passed along, He noticed a man blind from his birth.

His disciples asked Him, Rabbi, who sinned, this man or his parents, that he should be born blind?

Jesus answered It was not that this man or his parents sinned, but he was born blind in order that the workings of God should be manifested (displayed and illustrated) in him.

When He had said this, *He spat on the ground and made clay (mud) with His saliva, and He spread it [as ointment] on the man's eyes.*

And *He said to him, Go, wash in the Pool of Siloam—which means Sent. So he went and washed, and came back seeing.* (John 9:1–3, 6–7 AMPC)

Jesus's saliva had divine healing power as He is the author of life but then why did He mix it with mud? Shouldn't His saliva be enough to heal the blind or just His word? Yes, His word is enough to heal and even raise the dead as He demonstrated in many other instances (Matthew 8:5–13, John 11:39–44 AMPC). But in this instance, Jesus was demonstrating to the believers that they have medicine and medical help available for recovery from illnesses if their faith is small, but over and above these, they have the divine power in the name of Jesus to get healing and cure for ailments that science has no answers for or will ever have.

Jesus showed the importance of consent and follow-up action in faith.

If you read the accounts of healings that Jesus performed, you will notice that healings were by the way or an outcome of His love and compassion for those who were suffering. He went about preaching the kingdom of God not healing all and sundry. Most cases of healing happened when someone brought an unhealthy person to Jesus for healing or the sick themselves asked Jesus to heal them. Isn't that what we do naturally by taking someone sick to the doctor or meeting the doctor when we are unwell ourselves? Now the doctor not only has your consent but also your trust to diagnose the ailment and prescribe medicine.

In the instance when the blind beggar screamed and shrieked to get the attention of Jesus, He eventually asked the blind man what he wanted. Jesus could very well see that the beggar was blind, and certainly, he was not shouting to get money from Jesus as the beggar addressed Jesus with His lineage (people knew that the Messiah would come from the line of David). Here, Jesus was showing the importance of consent and faith on the part of the one needing healing.

> As He came near to Jericho, it occurred that a blind man was sitting by the roadside begging.
> And *he shouted, saying, Jesus, Son of David, take pity and have mercy on me!*
> But those who were in front reproved him, telling him to keep quiet; yet he screamed and shrieked so much the more, Son of David, take pity and have mercy on me!
> Then Jesus stood still and ordered that he be led to Him; and when he came near, *Jesus asked him,*
> *What do you want Me to do for you?* He said, Lord, let me receive my sight!
> And *Jesus said to him, Receive your sight! Your faith* (your trust and confidence that spring from your faith in God) *has healed you.*
> And instantly he received his sight and began to follow Jesus, recognizing, praising, and honoring God; and all the people, when they saw it, praised God. (Luke 18:35, 38–43 AMPC)

I have learned this lesson over time that when I have prayed for people without their asking for help, the person has very rarely received healing. But whenever there was a genuine and desperate call for a prayer of healing, the miracle happened, provided the follow-up action in faith was taken by the person after prayer. I had developed asthma back in India due to smoking for several years, but even after quitting for several years, the asthma had not gone away. I prayed for complete healing from asthma but did not take the follow-up action in faith as I kept going to my inhaler when I felt breathless. So I kept the inhaler as a backup just in case prayer did not work. Then, one day I realized where I was missing it and after praying for complete freedom from asthma, I threw away all the inhalers that were in my home (from the medicine closet, car, office bag, and my wife's purse). Now, my consent to Jesus to heal me by praying in His name met with my action in faith to throw away the backup plan, and the healing was permanent. The blind beggar threw away his backup plan as he knew very well that after going to Jesus to ask for help, he would not be able to go back to begging from the rich Pharisees and Sadducees of the times who did not recognize Jesus as the Messiah and opposed Him. Everyone has a measure of faith, and they must use it accordingly. I still use medical help in areas where my faith has still not developed, but as I exercise my faith muscle daily, I get bigger results in my life.

Jesus showed the importance of faith on the part of the person needing healing.

Faith is the cornerstone of achieving miracles in every area of our lives, including health. Even the medical profession recognizes the value of faith in healing and makes provision for prayer rooms in hospitals and allows patients to get their pastors to visit and pray for them. Some people say that faith-based healing works like placebos. A placebo can be roughly defined as a sham medical treatment. Common placebos include inert tablets (like sugar pills), inert injections (like saline), sham surgery, and other procedures. Placebos are popular because they can sometimes produce relief through psychological mechanisms (a phenomenon known as the "placebo effect"). They can affect how patients perceive their condition and encourage the body's chemical processes for relieving pain and a few other symptoms but have no impact on the disease itself.

Faith in Jesus is not a placebo effect as it may or may not relieve the person immediately of the symptoms of the ailment, but the healing is done the moment faith is released in His name.

> And Jesus said to him, Go your way; your faith has healed you. And at once he received his sight and accompanied Jesus on the road. (Mark 10:52 AMPC)

> And He said to her, Daughter, your faith (your trust and confidence in Me, springing from faith in God) has restored you to health. Go in (into) peace and be continually healed and freed from your [distressing bodily] disease. (Mark 5:34 AMPC)

The manifestation of healing and its continuity are dependent on the person continuing in faith by taking follow-up actions without doubting. Doubt is the killer of the miracle! Even Jesus could not do any miracles of healing in His own hometown where people lacked faith.

> But Jesus said to them, A prophet is not without honor (deference, reverence) except in his [own] country and among [his] relatives and in his [own] house.
> And *He was not able to do even one work of power there*, except that He laid His hands on a few sickly people [and] cured them.
> And *He marveled because of their unbelief* (their lack of faith in Him). And He went about among the surrounding villages and continued teaching. (Mark 6:4–6 AMPC)

Jesus displayed the healing power in Himself.
Jesus didn't mince words when He claimed Himself to be the Life and had the authority to lay it down and take it up again.

Jesus said to him, *I am the Way and the Truth and the Life*; no one comes to the Father except by (through) Me. (John 14:6 AMPC)

Jesus said to her, *I am [Myself] the Resurrection and the Life*. Whoever believes in (adheres to, trusts in, and relies on) Me, although he may die, yet he shall live. (John 11:25 AMPC)

For this [reason] the Father loves Me, *because I lay down My [own] life—to take it back again.*

No one takes it away from Me. On the contrary, I lay it down voluntarily. [I put it from Myself.] *I am authorized and have power to lay it down (to resign it) and I am authorized and have power to take it back again*. These are the instructions (orders) which I have received [as My charge] from My Father. (John 10:17–18 AMPC)

What is the best place to go if the engine of your car starts failing or goes dead? The next-door mechanic may be able to fix smaller issues, but the manufacturer guarantees to either fix it or replace it. People may not believe in Jesus, but when it comes to a life-and-death situation for themselves or their loved ones, then they know that there is no other name they can call out to. As someone has said, "If you don't believe in the healing power of Jesus, then you haven't gotten sick enough!"

The time I started writing this book in the last week of December 2023, I developed a severe toothache. The dentist had told me that due to my habit of grinding my teeth while asleep (bruxism), the teeth will keep breaking unless I use the night guard before going to bed. I tried but gave up on wearing the night guard as it's just awful to stuff something in your mouth and be able to sleep. The pain got worse and became unbearable at times as I kept praying for healing from bruxism and relief from pain. Finally, I decided to go to the dentist, but before going there, I prayed that there should not be any cavity or need for a root canal. The X-ray did not show any cavity so, a root canal was ruled out. The doctor concluded that there could be a crack in the tooth, and the only solution was to pull the tooth out.

A couple of weeks passed, but the pain would not go away, and it kept me awake at night, shooting from the tooth all that way to my temple. I used this time of pain and sleepless nights to pray for long hours. One day, the pain was so severe that I told Jesus to either provide me complete relief from pain or call me home. I fought with Him in prayer and told Him that I would not be able to write this book convincingly if He did not heal me. I had gotten sick enough to scream and fight with Him for my healing, forgetting even the fact that the moment I had asked Jesus for a complete restoration, He was working to get the root cause fixed instead of doing a patchwork of restoring that particular tooth that was hurting. The next day, I went back to Him in repentance of my behavior, and He lovingly revealed that He was allowing my pain to continue so that my body would get trained to not grind the teeth while I was asleep and unable to release my faith. I understood that, but the pain was so severe that the next day, I told Him that I would not continue to write this book unless He gave me my miracle and complete relief from this excruciating pain.

Then at 7:00 a.m. on January 11, 2024, while I was asleep, Jesus picked me up in His loving embrace, taking me to heaven hugging and kissing me on my forehead and face. He said, "Is there anything too hard for me?"

After this out-of-body experience, I said, "Lord, I will not need any other miracle in my life to continue doing what you have asked me to do for you." I will finish this book, and anything else Jesus asks me to do even if that means I have to pull this tooth out and go on serving the Lord. No suffering in my life will ever cause me to sin doubting Him. I was relieved of the intense pain, but the discomfort continued for a couple of months. During this time, hands were laid on me by my pastor and a visiting pastor, Nancy Dufresne, for freedom from bruxism. God healed me of bruxism, and when I finally went to get my tooth extracted, the dentist was surprised to see the tooth split in two from the middle. And still I was without pain. Sometimes, when your faith is not enough to get the healing that you need, you can use other people's faith.

> Likewise, you who are younger *and* of lesser rank, be subject to the elders (the ministers and spiritual guides of the church) [giving them due respect and yielding to their counsel]. Clothe (apron) yourselves, all of you, with humility [as the garb of a servant, so that its covering cannot possibly be stripped from you, with freedom from pride and arrogance] toward one another. For God sets Himself against the proud (the insolent, the overbearing, the disdainful, the presumptuous, the boastful) [and He opposes, frustrates, and defeats them], but gives grace (favor, blessing) to the humble. (1 Peter 5:5 AMPC)

Jesus gave believers the authority to use His Name to heal.
I have heard believers say, "If it is His will then I will be healed," or they would beg God to heal them. That's like saying to your parents when you are sick that if it is your will then take me to the doctor. Such a parent would only be completely given to evil if their child had to beg them for help while in pain and suffering.

"If you then, evil as you are, know how to give good and advantageous gifts to your children, how much more will your Father Who is in heaven [perfect as He is] give good and advantageous things to those who keep on asking Him!" (Matthew 7:11 AMPC).

First, we need to understand that sickness is not from God as He cannot give something that He does not have. God is love and He has only life in Himself. That is what He can give to all His children as per His many promises in the Bible.

> Bless (affectionately, gratefully praise) the Lord,
> O my soul, and forget not [one of] all His benefits—

> Who forgives [every one of] all your iniquities, Who heals [each one of] all your diseases. (Psalm 103:2–3 AMPC)

Sickness and disease come from the devil when we open the door to him through the sins that we commit from time to time. But the moment we repent, God forgives us and is willing to heal us if we release our faith for healing in prayer.

> Confess to one another therefore your faults (your slips, your false steps, your offenses, your sins) and pray [also] for one another, that you may be healed and restored [to a spiritual tone of mind and heart]. The earnest (heartfelt, continued) prayer of a righteous man makes tremendous power available [dynamic in its working]. (James 5:16 AMPC)

The best part is that believers have the authority and power to get healing and also impart healing to others because Jesus gave that authority to those who believe in Him.

> THEN JESUS called together the Twelve [apostles] and gave them power and authority over all demons, and to cure diseases,
> And He sent them out to announce and preach the kingdom of God and to bring healing. (Luke 9:1–2 AMPC)

The problem is that believers have either not understood the promises of healing in the Bible or have just given up the fight for their rightful inheritance. It's like carrying the credit card that your dad gave you in your pocket, but unless you swipe it, the money keeps sitting in your dad's bank account. Some believers think that this authority that Jesus gave was only to His twelve initial disciples. If that were so, then Christianity should have finished some 1,900 years ago after the death of all these disciples and Jesus would not have said this: "I assure you, most solemnly I tell you, if *anyone steadfastly believes in Me*, he will himself be able to do the things that I do, and he will do even greater things than these because I go to the Father" (John 14:12 AMPC).

It's up to us if we want to value this freely given power and authority to lead abundant lives and bless others or disregard it.

"Cure the sick, raise the dead, cleanse the lepers, drive out demons. Freely (without pay) you have received, freely (without charge) give" (Matthew 10:8 AMPC).

Jesus gave you the power to raise the dead.

One of the biggest fears that people have is death. We see death all around us all our lives but are so fearful even at the thought of it coming to us or our loved ones. But if believers look at death from the lens of God, then it's just passing on from one phase of life to the next one, which is most glorious as it is with Jesus Himself and all our born-again loved ones who have preceded us into everlasting life in heaven. Look at what Jesus said to his disciples:

> In My Father's house there are many dwelling places (homes). If it were not so, I would have told you; for I am going away to prepare a place for you.
>
> And when (if) I go and make ready a place for you, I will come back again and will take you to Myself, that where I am you may be also.
>
> And [to the place] where I am going, you know the way.
>
> Thomas said to Him, Lord, we do not know where You are going, so how can we know the way?
>
> Jesus said to him, I am the Way and the Truth and the Life; no one comes to the Father except by (through) Me.

Even though we know that death is not to be feared, but still, the pain of losing loved ones is real, especially if death is premature. For this reason, Jesus gave us the power to raise the dead to help grieving family members if they are inconsolable. This is the most powerful thing that a believer can have but it's also the most difficult thing to have. A believer will need to have a "raw bulldog" faith in the name of Jesus and courage to even think of attempting it unless the move of the Holy Spirit comes upon people like the instance when many saints rose from the dead at the resurrection of Jesus (Matthew 27:52–53 AMPC).

There are several accounts in the Bible about people raising the dead before Jesus came to earth (Elijah in 1 Kings 17:17–22 and Elisha in 2 Kings 4:32–35 AMPC) and after Jesus ascended to heaven (Apostle Paul in Acts 20:9, 10 and Peter in Acts 9:36–41 AMPC), besides Jesus Himself raising the dead on three occasions. Apart from Jesus, who has the power in Himself to bring life, the other people were ordinary folks like you and me, but with a pure, unadulterated faith in the living God the Father and His Son Jesus Christ. The present-day testimonies of people being raised from the dead are many, and to quote one is by David Hogan who has his ministry in Mexico. God has allowed him to be present on twenty-eight occasions where the dead were raised to life.[4] The gist of it is that Jesus gave us the authority and power to raise the dead in His Name and that power is working even today, whether we accept it or not is up to us.

"And as you go, preach, saying, The kingdom of heaven is at hand! Cure the sick, *raise the dead*, cleanse the lepers, drive out demons. Freely (without pay) you have received, freely (without charge) give" (Matthew 10:7–8 AMPC).

Why has this power to heal the sick and raise the dead been working only with very few preachers and evangelists in present times? I would think the main reason is a lack of faith in the body of Christ.

> He said to them, Because of the littleness of your faith [that is, your lack of firmly relying on trust]. For truly I say to you, if you have faith [that is living] like a grain of mustard seed, you can say to this mountain, Move from here to yonder place,

---

[4] https://freedom-ministries.us/post-portfolio/david-and-debbie-hogan/

and it will move; and nothing will be impossible to you. (Matthew 17:20 AMPC)

A religiously motivated suicide bomber has more faith, though misplaced in the evil one, than today's generation of Christians. The terrorist goes on to destroy lives along with their own life motivated by the rewards in their version of heaven.

> You are of your father, the devil, and it is your will to practice the lusts and gratify the desires [which are characteristic] of your father. He was a murderer from the beginning and does not stand in the truth, because there is no truth in him. When he speaks a falsehood, he speaks what is natural to him, for he is a liar [himself] and the father of lies and of all that is false. (John 8:44 AMPC)

But Jesus called believers to have abundant life here and now along with life eternal. Jesus commissioned believers to give life, not destroy it, whether their own or of others.

"The thief comes only in order to steal and kill and destroy. I came that they may have and enjoy life, and have it in abundance (to the full, till it overflows)" (John 10:10 AMPC).

Believer's Authority to Get Wealth

Poverty is a disease!
Someone may say you are being insensitive to the poor and less fortunate. Well, when the doctor tells you that you have cancer, do you turn back and say, "You are being insensitive"? Rather, you seek a doctor's help to get rid of the sickness.

The way the devil puts disease on you, it's the same way he puts poverty on you. Poverty is a state of mind rather than a function of how much money you have in your bank or lack of it.

Once, I was walking with a friend in the high-rise condominium where we lived in Bangalore, and seeing the slum right across from our condo, he said sympathetically how these people in the slums would be feeling looking at us leading rich and prosperous lives. I said to this well-meaning friend, "How did you conclude that they are poor, and we are rich? Rather they may be saying, 'How poor are these rich people who have everything but keep running around leading their lives in such a frenzy?'" Ahh, did you get the rub of it? Look at how Jesus defined poverty:

> LOOKING UP, [Jesus] saw the rich people putting their gifts into the treasury.
> And He saw also a poor widow putting in two mites (copper coins).
> And He said, Truly I say to you, *this poor widow has put in more than all of them*;
> For they all gave out of their abundance (their surplus); but she has contributed out of her lack and her want, putting in all that she had on which to live. (Luke 21:1–4 AMPC)

If you make fifty thousand dollars a month and donate five thousand, then you have given 10 percent, but if you make five thousand and donate all of it, then you have given 100 percent. The value of the amount given is the same, but how much the person gives or holds back and the motive behind giving is what makes them rich or poor.

The sight of women and children begging in India had always moved me and, at times, puzzled me. Every time I have given money to these people begging on the road, it has given me a good feeling but never satisfied me. After many years of wondering about this mixed emotion, I came to realize that unless these people are set free in their soul (mind, emotions, will) and body, they will keep on begging all their lives. Look at this study done in India:

> The study was conducted on all beggars begging at Saibaba Temple located in Kalyan City, under Mumbai Metropolitan Region, Maha-

rashtra. Total 113 (92 males and 21 females) beggars, were surveyed, clinically examined and treated. Of these 113 beggars, 70.80% were illiterate while 29.20% were literate. Surprisingly, one male beggar was a commerce graduate. One female beggar had voter identity and ration card. 44.25% beggars were alcoholic.85.84% beggars were having their family either broken or with problem. Of these 113 beggars, 110 (97.35%) were having one or more health problems. Majority of them i.e. 81(71.68%) were suffering from musculo-skeletal problems. Upper respiratory tract infections (20.91%), tuberculosis (07.08%) and leprosy (06.19%) were also seen prominently among them.[5]

This study shows that some of the issues that kept them in poverty are illiteracy, addictions, family problems, and health issues. None of these causes are beyond remedy, and the state does in varying measures address these from time to time, but the issue of poverty remains in India and many other countries of the world as the state does not always know or allow the souls of these people to be set free by the living Word of God in the Bible. As per Forbes, India ranks fifth among the top 10 economies of the world as of 2024 with Canada being tenth.[6] According to the United Nations Millennium Development Goals (MDG) program, 80 million people out of 1.2 billion Indians, roughly equal to 6.7 percent of India's population, lived below the poverty line of $1.25 per day and 84 percent of Indians lived on less than $6.85 per day in 2019.[7] Why has such

---

[5] https://www.worldwidejournals.com/international-journal-of-scientific-research-(IJSR)/recent_issues_pdf/2015/January/January_2015_1420283874__153.pdf

[6] https://www.forbesindia.com/article/explainers/top-10-largest-economies-in-the-world/86159/1

[7] https://en.wikipedia.org/wiki/Poverty_in_India#:~:text=Based%20on%202019's%20PPPs%20International,than%20%246.85%20per%20day%20in

a strong economy not been able to resolve the poverty issue, with 90 percent of the country in poverty making barely $200 a month? There's got to be something very wrong here for so many people leading such miserable lives as though blinded by some unseen force. Well, we know what that unseen blinding force is in people's lives that keeps them in a state of poverty.

"For the god of this world has blinded the unbelievers' minds [that they should not discern the truth], preventing them from seeing the illuminating light of the Gospel of the glory of Christ (the Messiah), Who is the Image and Likeness of God" (2 Corinthians 4:4 AMPC).

But the good news of the Gospel of Christ has the power to set people free from bondage to poverty be it financial, health-related, or in relationships. Let's look at how believers can break the bondage of poverty and lead financially blessed lives.

Prosperity is a covenant of God.

A covenant is a written agreement or promise usually under seal between two or more parties, especially for the performance of some action. Now look at what the Almighty God of this whole wide universe said to you and me who are the second party to the agreement: "But you shall [earnestly] remember the Lord your God, for it is He Who gives you power to get wealth, that He may establish His covenant which He swore to your fathers, as it is this day" (Deuteronomy 8:18 AMPC).

We have the easy part in the covenant act, that of earnestly remembering Him (reading and meditating on His Word), and God does the difficult part of giving us His divine power to get wealth. Also, the word mentioned in this promise is *wealth*, which the dictionary defines as "an abundance of valuable possessions or money." Have you ever had a wealth manager helping you with your money? Most people will never need wealth managers in their lifetime. But here God promises wealth, and you don't need wealth to just get by the month paying your bills. Most of us can very well take care of our basic necessities of life (food, shelter, and clothing); and we don't need to exercise our faith on a daily basis for that. But to get wealth, we very well will need the hand of God working mightily in our lives. So why do most of the believers live just to make a living? Here's why: *Covenant needs the "keeping."*

Just the act of getting into a marriage covenant with your spouse will not keep your marriage going well and forever. Both parties will need to keep the covenant of marriage by loving, serving, helping, and abiding with each other all the days of their lives. In the case of the covenant of prosperity between God and you, who has the easy part? But let's see who misses it all the time:

> Know, recognize, and understand therefore that the Lord your God, He is God, the faithful God, Who keeps covenant and steadfast love and mercy *with those who love Him and keep His commandments*, to a thousand generations,
>
> And repays those who hate Him to their face, by destroying them; He will not be slack to him who hates Him but will requite him to his face. (Deuteronomy 7:9–10 AMPC)

You see here that we are the ones who miss it by breaking the covenant act of loving Him and keeping His commandments. As I wrote this book, I remembered the fact that I had missed my covenant act of tithing on the sale of our property in India in 2017. God had miraculously brought about the sale of our property during that time when the government of India had demonetized five hundred and one thousand rupee banknotes, and the real estate market had dropped drastically. But God kept His covenant of blessing on us, and a precious friend of ours bought our house at a fair market value without considering the market conditions. My wife and I decided to make up for this miss and went on to tithe as per the sale value of the house.

Am I a perfect man? Not even by any stretch of the imagination. But I am in covenant with the perfect God who keeps His covenant always. God kept His covenant with Isaac and blessed the seed he sowed a hundred times. I am a child of the same God and believe His hundredfold blessing on the seed that we have sown as a family all our lives.

> Then Isaac sowed seed in that land and received in the same year a hundred times as much as he had planted, and the Lord favored him with blessings. (Genesis 26:12 AMPC)

Covenant needs the "obedience."

Obedience is one virtue that has eroded the most over time. Gone are the days when mothers could spank their kids for disobeying them. In this part of the world, you can't even think of doing that, or else your kids could be taken away and put in foster care. The Bible is crystal clear about the virtue of "obedience" as a condition to receiving all of the blessings of God including prosperity.

"Now therefore, if you will obey My voice in truth and keep My covenant, then you shall be My own peculiar possession and treasure from among and above all peoples; for all the earth is Mine" (Exodus 19:5 AMPC).

When it comes to prosperity, God has put in place these covenant acts of obedience for his children:

Tithing.

> Bring all the tithes (*the whole tenth of your income*) into the storehouse, that there may be food in My house, and prove Me now by it, says the Lord of hosts, if I will not open the windows of heaven for you and pour you out a blessing, that there shall not be room enough to receive it. (Malachi 3:10 AMPC)

Believers are called to give back 10 percent of all that God has blessed them with financially to their local Church and not to any charitable organization or someone in need. Giving to any other cause is something that you can do on top of the tithe that you have put in your local Church. This needs to be a continuous act of obedience throughout your life in the same manner as God keeps blessing you all your life.

Look at the later part of the verse, which is the response of the covenant-keeping God if we obey our part of the covenant.

"And prove Me now by it, says the Lord of hosts, if I will not open the windows of heaven for you and pour you out a blessing, that there shall not be room enough to receive it."

Can you even imagine what it means for the Almighty God, the creator of this unfathomable universe, to open the windows of heaven on you? Such a financial blessing is something you can never generate by your work or business in your lifetime.

Sowing and reaping.

"Do not be deceived, God is not mocked [He will not allow Himself to be ridiculed, nor treated with contempt nor allow His precepts to be scornfully set aside]; *for whatever a man sows, this and this only is what he will reap*" (Galatians 6:7 AMP).

Sowing is what we give over and above the tithes to the local Church. We can sow into the Church or any other charitable organization or a person. Whatever we sow is exactly what we get back. If you sow money, you will get back money. If you sow love, you will reap love. If you sow unforgiveness, you get back unforgiveness. The biblical principle of "sowing and reaping" applies to all the areas of our lives.

> For he who sows to his own flesh (lower nature, sensuality) will from the flesh reap decay and ruin and destruction, but he who sows to the Spirit will from the Spirit reap eternal life. (Galatians 6:8 AMPC)

> As I myself have seen, those who plow iniquity and sow trouble and mischief reap the same. (Job 4:8 AMPC)

Sowing in good ground is extremely important to receiving a rich harvest. The farmer sows seed in good, fertilized ground rather than rocky ground or one infested with weeds. We, as a family, have availed most of the opportunities to sow into men and women of God who are called to do the work of God. That's good ground because they are given to the work of saving souls for God. You may decide to sow into a charitable organization that is into helping sick people, and that's perfectly fine. But for us saving souls from eternal damnation is more important than saving bodies in the here and now.

Reaping does not precede sowing. Many people think that once I have enough, then I will sow. If all the farmers start thinking that way, then there will not be much food on our tables. Harvest comes in due season after the sowing has been done, and the seed is in good ground for some time.

"Then will He give you rain for the seed with which you sow the soil, and bread grain from the produce of the ground, and it will be rich and plentiful. In that day your cattle will feed in large pastures" (Isaiah 30:23 AMPC).

You must die first to the urge to retain that thing that you have decided in your heart to sow. Only then can you be joyful in giving and in due season expect to reap a rich harvest.

"You foolish man! Every time you plant seed, you sow something that does not come to life [germinating, springing up, and growing] unless it dies first" (1 Corinthians 15:36 AMPC).

Once you have taken that leap of faith in sowing your seed in good ground, thereafter, God will keep giving you seed to sow till the time you don't give up sowing.

"And [God] Who provides seed for the sower and bread for eating will also provide and multiply your [resources for] sowing and increase the fruits of your righteousness [which manifests itself in active goodness, kindness, and charity]" (2 Corinthians 9:10 AMPC).

Now, here's the clincher! The bountiful harvest from God that your finite mind cannot fathom.

> Give, and it will be given to you. They will pour into your lap a good measure—pressed down, shaken together, and running over [with no space

left for more]. For with the standard of measurement you use [when you do good to others], it will be measured to you in return. (Luke 6:38 AMP)

But you will again need to appropriate all His bountiful blessings by faith and not giving up as you wait for the harvest.

"Let us not grow weary or become discouraged in doing good, for at the proper time we will reap *if we do not give in*" (Galatians 6:9 AMP).

Believer's Authority to Be Peaceful

Peace, as defined in the *Oxford English Dictionary*, means "Freedom from anxiety, disturbance (emotional, mental, or spiritual), or inner conflict; calm, tranquility."[8] But in reality, to be completely free from all our emotions of fear and anxiety will mean we must be dead.

The Bible is not unreasonable to define peace in such a foolish manner. It recognizes that you can never get rid of your God-given emotions either while you are alive on earth or when you are in heaven because God does not want people here on earth or in heaven walking like zombies.

You get peace by casting your anxieties and worries on the source of life and the Prince of peace, Jesus Christ.

> *Casting all your cares [all your anxieties, all your worries, and all your concerns, once and for all] on Him*, for He cares about you [with deepest affection, and watches over you very carefully]. (1 Peter 5:7 AMP)
>
> *For to us a Child shall be born, to us a Son shall be given*; And the government shall be upon His

---

[8] https://www.oed.com/dictionary/peace_n?tl=true

shoulder, *And His name shall be called* Wonderful Counselor, Mighty God, Everlasting Father, *Prince of Peace.* (Isaiah 9:6 AMP)

How do you cast your cares on Jesus? By believing in Him wholeheartedly and meditating on His Word. Jesus said, "Come to Me, all you who labor and are heavy-laden and overburdened, and I will cause you to rest. [I will ease and relieve and refresh your souls.]" (Matthew 11:28 AMPC).

When Jesus said come to me, then that does not mean that we have to go to heaven to have peace. What that means is that we need to go to the Word (the Bible), to find rest as Jesus is the Word.

And the Word (Christ) became flesh (human, incarnate) and tabernacled (fixed His tent of flesh, lived awhile) among us; and we [actually] saw His glory (His honor, His majesty), such glory as an only begotten son receives from his father, full of grace (favor, loving-kindness) and truth. (John 1:14 AMPC)

After you feed on the living Word of God continuously you will be able to live in complete peace irrespective of the circumstances surrounding your life. You will be at peace amidst the turmoils of life, for Jesus said,

I have told you these things, so that in Me you may have [perfect] peace and confidence. In the world you have tribulation and trials and distress and frustration; but be of good cheer [take courage; be confident, certain, undaunted]! For I have overcome the world. [I have deprived it of power to harm you and have conquered it for you.] (John 16:33 AMPC)

A life completely surrendered to the Author and Creator of life itself soars and floats above the turbulence of life's circumstances. It helps you to live by faith, not by sight.

"For we walk by faith, not by sight [living our lives in a manner consistent with our confident belief in God's promises]" (2 Corinthians 5:7 AMP).

When we were moving from India to Canada without a clue where we were going to live or what we would be doing for a living; we were moving in faith in our Lord who had kept us in His care all our lives without even a day going by when we did not have food on our table, roof on our heads, and clothes to wear. We moved by faith not by sight, in complete peace and childlike joy of the glorious future ahead of us in a new and beautiful country.

People may have all the wealth and health, but if there is no peace, then everything else is meaningless. The abandonment of childlike beliefs as we grow up is the most fatal blow to peace that man will ever experience. The early twentieth-century philosopher, G. K. Chesterton, rightly stated,

> The new rebel is a skeptic, and will not trust anything…but therefore he can never be really a revolutionary. For all denunciation implies a moral doctrine of some kind… Therefore the modern man in revolt has become practically useless for all purposes of revolt. By rebelling against everything he has lost his right to rebel against anything… There is a thought that stops thought. That is the only thought that ought to be stopped.[9]

I remember as a child, we had a bush in our verandah with lots of leaves. My pants and shirt pockets were always stuffed with a stack of these leaves as I believed that these were actual currency notes. I went about like a king giving money to imaginary people

---

[9] https://marcjsims.com/2015/09/21/nietzsche-is-dead-god/

and buying whatever I wanted with it, cars, airplanes, houses, and countries. We had a chest of drawers, and the top-left side drawer was my brother's, and the right side was mine. Mine was always full of toy cars, machines taken out of toys to build helicopters, and stacks of leaf cash. I was everything that I wanted to be—a pilot, a Formula 1 driver, a business tycoon, a president, a king! Isn't that how the King of kings, the God Almighty made you and me in the beginning?

> So God created man in His own image, in the image and likeness of God He created him; male and female He created them. And God blessed them [granting them certain authority] and said to them, "Be fruitful, multiply, and fill the earth, and subjugate it [putting it under your power]; and rule over (dominate) the fish of the sea, the birds of the air, and every living thing that moves upon the earth." (Genesis 1:27–28 AMP)

But then life happened to me as I grew older, reasoning took over dreams and imaginations. The school taught that I evolved from a monkey. Earthly father marred the image of a caring and loving heavenly Father. The world snatched the child out of me and killed my simple childlike faith and belief. It took a long twenty-five years to get back my childlike faith in the loving heavenly Father who formed me in my mother's womb.

> For You formed my innermost parts;
> You knit me [together] in my mother's womb.
> I will give thanks and praise to You, for I am fear-
>   fully and wonderfully made;
> Wonderful are Your works,
> And my soul knows it very well. (Psalm 139:13–
>   14 AMP)

My brothers and sisters in Christ, you must not lose your childlike belief in the loving Father who sent His only Son to die for you and me so that we may enjoy the fullness of His blessings in the here and now and for life everlasting in His embrace. Jesus loves you as you are. He did not come into the world to start another religion but to restore our relationship with the Father and give us abundant life! It's never too late to give your life to Jesus and start living the *ironclad, powerful, surefire* life in Him as your Lord and Savior.

About the Author

Rohit Phillips is an entrepreneur, business manager, author, and photographer. Born in India, Rohit is now settled in Canada with his wife and two daughters. Rohit loves wildlife photography, and it's his dream to travel to the farthest corners of the world to shoot wildlife and be a fisher of men for Jesus Christ.

Printed in the USA
CPSIA information can be obtained
at www.ICGtesting.com
LVHW040006210924
791672LV00001B/63